PRAISE FOR *Miracl*

"After a search that proved to be cathartic emotionally, Biegel may have found the truth, if not the ball."   —*New York Times*

"The adventure documented in *Miracle Ball* is ample evidence that Biegel is the Magellan of literary searchers. But *Miracle Ball* isn't just about the journey. What Biegel also captures are the dynamics of the relationships between fathers and sons, between Americans and their national pastime, between history and mythology. *Miracle Ball* is a poignant, funny, and important addition to the baseball canon."   —Jeremy Schaap, *New York Times* bestselling author of *Cinderella Man* and *Triumph*

"The narrative is peppered with riveting oral reminiscences of the game and passages from eminent sportswriters like Red Smith, filled   riting
so c   this
surp   the
wall   *views*

"Mo   . . .
you   *ews*

"Bie   rom
run   e to
hav   old
nur   ges
turn   out
an   *zette*

"Ultimately, the story of his mission is a heartwarming tale of the lifelong bonds baseball can create between father and son."

—*Montreal Gazette*

"Do you love gripping mysteries, hinging on crime forensics? Historical novels? Self-help books? Tales of redemption? Fantasy? Baseball? Stories of faith and the power of family? In *Miracle Ball*, author Brian Biegel has pulled off a minor miracle, combining all those books in 227 fast-moving pages." —*Las Cruces Sun-News*

"A fast-paced, fascinating tale that combines shoe leather, high-tech forensics and some healthy dollops of luck. . . . [This] book is a home run." —*Anderson Independent-Mail*

MIRACLE BALL

MIRACLE BALL

My Hunt for
the Shot Heard 'Round the World

Brian Biegel

WITH
Peter Thomas Fornatale

THREE RIVERS PRESS

NEW YORK

Originally published in hardcover in the United States by Crown Publishers,
an imprint of the Crown Publishing Group, a division of Random House, Inc.,
in 2009.

Library of Congress Cataloging-in-Publication Data

Biegel, Brian.
Miracle ball: my hunt for the Shot heard 'round the world / Brian Biegel; with
Peter Thomas Fornatale.
p.   cm.
1. Biegel, Brian. 2. Thomson, Bobby, 1923– 3. Brooklyn Dodgers (Baseball
team)—History. 4. New York Giants (Baseball team)—History. 5. World
Series (Baseball) (1951) 6. Baseball—United States—History. 7. Baseball—
Collectors and collecting—United States. 8. Baseball—United States—
History. 9. Baseball—Equipment and supplies—History. 10. Baseball—
Equipment and supplies—Collectors and collecting.

GV875.2 .B54 2009
796.357028/4 22   2009278419

ISBN 978-0-307-45269-6

Printed in the United States of America

Design by Level C

10 9 8 7 6 5 4 3 2 1

First Paperback Edition

To my mother, Sandy

Mom, I know you're reading this book, smiling, humbly telling those near you in heaven how so very proud you are of me. Well, I'm more proud of you. I'm the most fortunate person alive to have had a mother so honorable and caring as you. You saved me from myself when I needed you most. I believe that my love travels out of my heart and makes its way directly into your soul every moment of every day. Throughout your life you sacrificed your own happiness for your family's. Nary a person who came near you could ever walk away without feeling your warmth, kindness, compassion, and pure goodness. I felt it every day you were alive. There will never be an equal to you.

Contents

Prologue   "The Holy Grail of Sports"   xi

ONE   Brooklyn Boy   I

TWO   The Armoire   II

THREE   Dad vs. Lelands   25

FOUR   Esther   41

FIVE   "The Whole World Will Know You"   57

SIX   Searching for Eddie Logan   71

SEVEN   CSI: Polo Grounds   83

EIGHT   My Fifteen Minutes of Fame   101

NINE   Junk from the Attic   115

TEN   Dodger Daze   127

ELEVEN   "The Best Baseball Writer of
His Time"   137

TWELVE   Eyewitness   149

THIRTEEN   Private Detectives   161

FOURTEEN   The Angel   173

FIFTEEN   Fervor   181

SIXTEEN   The Three Helens   191

SEVENTEEN   Digging Up the Past   205

EIGHTEEN   It's Not About the Ball   211

NINETEEN   New Mexico   217

Epilogue   Faith   225

            Acknowledgments   229

"Nobody has the ball," Sims said. "The ball never turned up. Whoever once had the ball, it never surfaced. This is part of the whole—what? The mythology of the game."

—Don DeLillo, *Underworld*

Dodgers left fielder Andy Pafko watches the home run sail over his head. A newspaper editor inserted an arrow (in the 1950s), indicating the vicinity of the ball or the fan who caught it. *Hank Olen, courtesy of the New York Daily News*

"The Holy Grail of Sports"

Wednesday, October 3, 1951

The sun hung over the first-base side of the Polo Grounds, reflecting off the apartment buildings that lined Harlem River Drive and onto the open end of the stadium behind the left-field stands. The clock in center field read 3:58.

The details of the play itself are familiar to most baseball fans. Branca had Thomson down in the count 0-1, the result of a called strike right down the middle. It was the bottom of the ninth. Two men on base. The Giants trailed the Dodgers by two runs in the last game of a three-game playoff series. The winner would advance to the World Series against the New York Yankees. Out of the windup, Branca threw a fastball, high and tight. But this time Thomson, the lanky outfielder turned third baseman, was ready. He pulled the pitch to left field—a sinking line drive.

The fans in the lower portion of section 35 followed the flight of the ball. A photo captured the moment perfectly. There was an overweight, middle-aged man in a white T-shirt and a black jacket in the first row. Next to him was a buzz-cut teenager with thick-rimmed eyeglasses. A row above them stood a man with a handlebar mustache and a fedora. In the fourth row, a bushy-haired man stood with his arms stretched above his head and his mouth wide open.

The crowd's loyalties were evenly divided: The Dodgers fans prayed that the ball would somehow find its way into left fielder Andy Pafko's mitt; the Giants fans prayed that it wouldn't. The teams' rivalry—the oldest in professional sports—dated back all the way to the nineteenth century, but it had never seen a moment like this.

The prayers of the home team's fans were answered: Thomson had hit a home run; the Giants won the pennant. Thomson's blast became known as the Shot Heard 'Round the World.

As for the baseball itself, that's been a mystery ever since. Just after the ball cleared the wall, it bounced out of a fan's glove and ricocheted seven feet to the left—straight into the hands of a person who would ensure that its fate would not be discovered for more than fifty years.

IT IS THE most iconic moment in the history of American sports—Bobby Thomson's game-winning home run to clinch the 1951 pennant for the Giants at the Polo Grounds. It's been mythologized by everyone from sportswriters and broadcasters to literary giants like John Steinbeck, Jack Kerouac, and Don DeLillo. There have been equally dramatic home runs, but none have had the lasting cultural impact of the Shot Heard 'Round the World.

But as obsessively documented and frequently relived as that moment was, something happened that day that remains a mystery. As Bobby Thomson rounded the bases and broadcaster Russ Hodges so memorably shouted, "The Giants win the pennant! The Giants win the pennant!" the central artifact of the play—the ball itself—landed in the left-field seats and then . . . vanished.

While much has been written and said about the Thomson home run and its impact, remarkably little is known about what happened to the actual ball. It is one of sport's greatest mysteries. Legendary sportswriter Vic Ziegel has called the Thomson ball "the Holy Grail of sports." Over the past fifty years, several people have claimed to own it (often motivated by an exploding memorabilia market that has seen other well-known home-run balls fetch millions of dollars at auction), but all of their claims have been disproved. The president of one prestigious auction house has estimated the odds of locating the ball at an astronomical 1 in 200 million. Similarly, every baseball historian I spoke with told me that there was no way to learn what really happened to it.

Fortunately for me, they were wrong.

This is the story of my two-year quest to solve the mystery that was supposed to be unsolvable. Several years ago, my father realized that he might have the famous missing baseball, and what began as a way to help my dad became, frankly, an obsessive hunt. It's a journey that brought me from an auction house on Long Island to the National Baseball Hall of Fame in Cooperstown, New York, to Bobby Thomson's ranch-style home in New Jersey, to a forensics lab in Northern Long Island, to a dusty oil field in Texas, and ultimately to a spot on a quiet graveled road in New Mexico that was just about the last place I ever expected to be.

What kept me going was not simply the desire to unravel this legendary sports mystery. Like life itself, my search became all about the journey. Along the way, I met an incredible cast of characters: a celebrated sportswriter who has made a career out of writing about the Thomson ball; a crazed Dodgers fan who slept inside the Polo Grounds the night before the game; a retired NYPD detective who found an important clue hidden (in plain sight) in an old photo; a baseball fanatic whose uncanny memory provided a crucial piece of the puzzle; two men from New Jersey who shared a seemingly astounding tale that turned out to fit precisely with the other evidence; and many others.

It had been more than half a century since Thomson's home run clinched the 1951 National League pennant, but everywhere I turned, it seemed as if there was another person telling a passionate story about the home run, or another eminent author or director who used it as a backdrop in his work. The response became overwhelming when the *New York Daily News* ran a story on my search (in fact, it was one of the longest non-news features in the history of the paper).

Despite being a lifelong baseball fan, only in exploring this mystery did I come to fully appreciate what that game, and what those two teams, meant to baseball fans, and to New Yorkers of that era. As people told their stories, I began to understand why grown men cried in public over the game's outcome; why schoolchildren schemed to follow the contest during their classes; why a young deli worker—now the owner of the New York Mets—was so startled by Thomson's home run against his beloved Dodgers that he sliced off a piece of his pinkie finger while making a salami sandwich; why a Marine in a bunker in Korea, a die-hard Giants fan surreptitiously listening to the game on Armed Forces Radio, became so excited when he heard Russ Hodges's call that he accidentally shot off his rifle, spurring a firefight with the enemy; and why a little boy watching the home run on TV felt so inspired by the miracle that something was born inside him—his faith in God. He later became a renowned monsignor in the Catholic Church and team chaplain of the New York Jets. Bobby Thomson's moment was the stuff of flashbulb memories for millions.

And for me, the quest became deeply personal as well. It was from my father, who grew up a short distance from Ebbets Field in Brooklyn, that I inherited my love of baseball; it was for my father that I set out on this mission, as I attempted to determine whether his ball really was the Shot Heard 'Round the World; and it was my father and mother whose unwavering encouragement gave me the strength and confidence I needed to persevere during the darkest period of my life.

Recovering from a bitter divorce and struggling with crippling depression and anxiety, I saw in the Thomson ball a way out, a

way to regain my old sense of self. But depression is a powerful op-
ponent and not one I was able to defeat on my own. What spurred
me on was the love and unconditional support my parents showed
me. As it turned out, this pursuit was the best kind of therapy I
could ever want: Set a goal for yourself and work toward it—and
refuse to be told you can't do it. I have come to believe that this
mission saved my life.

And for all the amazing things that happened during the
search—the series of exceedingly unlikely twists of fate that brought
me to my goal, the joy I saw in my mom's face as I got closer to the
truth, the opportunity to bring closure to my dad's million-dollar
dream, and the long-buried secret that lay at the end of the trail—I
have come to regard this famous piece of cowhide as a miracle ball.

MIRACLE BALL

Jack Biegel (Dad) warms up for the class D baseball Hopkinsville Hoppers in 1950. *From the author's collection*

Brooklyn Boy

Wednesday, October 3, 1951

For Jack Biegel and his fellow Brooklyn Dodgers fans, the 1951 season had been joyous and painful at the same time. Joyous because the team spent so much of the year in first place. Painful because they coughed up a 13 ½-game lead and had to play a best-of-three series against the hated Giants to determine who would represent the National League in the World Series against the Yankees.

On the day of the deciding game, eighteen-year-old Jack needed to be in Manhattan for a job interview. There was a position open as a shipping clerk at a company in the Garment District. Much as he wanted to go to the Polo Grounds to see the Dodgers and Giants in person, he couldn't take the risk; the game didn't start until 1:20, and afterward he'd have to cover well over a hundred blocks to get down to his interview by five o'clock. But that didn't mean he had to miss watching the game. Every bar worth its salt had a television, the amazing new invention that meant you didn't need to be at the ballpark to see every pitch. So he left for Manhattan about five hours before his interview was slated to begin.

Getting off the subway at Twenty-third Street and Seventh Avenue, fifteen blocks south of where he needed to be, Jack ducked into an Irish pub on Twenty-fifth Street just in time to see Jackie Robinson single home Pee Wee Reese for the first run of the game. He stayed there for several innings, then began weaving his way through the streets of Manhattan, checking the score through various pub windows, growing excited as the Dodgers inched closer to the pennant.

By the eighth inning, he'd settled in at a dive bar on Sixth Avenue as he watched the Dodgers touch up the exhausted Sal Maglie for three runs. With the Dodgers now leading 4-1, he headed to the job interview, confident the game was over.

But a few blocks from his destination, he noticed a crowd gathering in front of a small bar on West Thirty-sixth Street. The Giants were mounting a comeback. Alvin Dark and Don Mueller hit back-to-back singles. Then Whitey Lockman doubled down the left-field line, scoring Dark to cut the lead to 4-2. Jack stood outside and watched through the front glass in the huddled mass of Dodgers and Giants fans who could not squeeze inside. They were all just moments away from witnessing the impossible. With two men on base and the Giants needing three runs to win it in the bottom of the ninth, Thomson hit a fast-sinking line drive over the head of outfielder Andy Pafko and into the first few rows of the left-field stands. The Giants, not the Dodgers, won the pennant.

It was a moment that made time stand still for young Jack. Giants fans screamed with raw emotion as Jack stood with his heart in his throat. Two men in the group started to cry. Never before had Jack seen grown men show this kind of public emotion.

To add insult to injury, Jack didn't get the job.

It was a bad day for Brooklynites all around.

MY MISSION TO find the Thomson ball never would have started if not for my father. Jack Biegel, born in Brooklyn in 1933, was one of the millions of people whose life was touched by Thomson's home run. Growing up so close to Ebbets Field, it's no surprise that he took to baseball in general—and the Dodgers in particular—pretty much from day one. Like every kid in Brooklyn, he dreamed of playing in the famed ballpark on Bedford Avenue.

Jack had a lot of natural athletic talent, especially when it came to baseball. A left-handed pitcher with a good fastball and a decent slider, he also had a sound bat and played a solid first base. He played high school ball at Tilden, where in 1947—as a husky freshman—he made local headlines by pitching five shutout innings and then hitting a game-winning home run to beat crosstown rival Jefferson High. Another man named Jackie spent that year making bigger headlines in Brooklyn. His last name, of course, was Robinson.

During his high school years, Dad worked part-time at his uncle Heshie's dry-cleaning store on East Twenty-first Street and Church Avenue—the heart of Flatbush. He made the pickups and drop-offs. Uncle Heshie was a tall, well-dressed man who usually wore a fedora, a sport jacket, and pegged pants. One day in 1949, he gave Jack a delivery assignment along with a knowing smile and a pat on the back. The yellow receipt had two words written on it: "The Duke."

Clutching three hangers of freshly pressed suits, Jack made a beeline for Bedford Avenue, just a few blocks from Ebbets, where Dodgers center fielder Duke Snider lived. When Snider arrived in Brooklyn in 1947, he was touted as a budding superstar, and he was in the midst of his first big season (he'd finish the year with 23 homers and 92 RBIs). My dad thought the Duke could be to the Dodgers what Joe DiMaggio was to the Yankees. He wanted to play it cool on this delivery, but by the time he reached Duke's place, he could barely contain himself.

Dad was greeted at the door by another Dodger star, Gil Hodges. Looking down the long foyer that led into the living room, he could see that he had caught Hodges, Snider, and Dodger first-base coach Jake Pitler—the first Jewish coach in the major leagues—in the middle of a game of cards. My dad waited anxiously as the Duke got up from the table and sauntered toward him. To the young teenager from Brooklyn, this broad-shouldered Californian with bright blue eyes, blond-streaked hair, and a bronzed tan seemed half politician, half movie star.

Jack Biegel (Dad) wearing his
Tilden High School baseball
jacket, circa 1947. *From the author's
collection*

The Duke was a good tipper, but he impressed my dad even more
with his kindness. Duke affectionately called him Kiddo and on
subsequent deliveries found out that Jack wanted to be a ballplayer
and encouraged him to follow his dream. Jack's desire to play professional ball grew by the day. Especially on the days when Uncle
Heshie gave him the yellow receipt with the two special words
marked on it.

BUT DAD'S DREAM hit a roadblock when his father lost his job at
the Washington Fruit Market down near Canal Street in Manhattan. He ended up dropping out of high school halfway through his
senior year to work for Heshie full-time. The money he made there
in tips really helped at home, and he figured he still might be able
to get a tryout with a minor league team at some point. The system

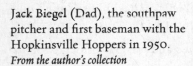

Jack Biegel (Dad), the southpaw pitcher and first baseman with the Hopkinsville Hoppers in 1950. *From the author's collection*

was different then. There were several hundred minor league affiliates across the country, extending all the way down from AAA to class D ball. And none of them cared if you had a high school diploma.

Every week my dad would pick up a copy of the *Sporting News,* the bible of baseball, at the newsstand near the IRT subway station on Eastern Parkway and Utica Avenue. He was a stats freak. He'd also check out the classified ads, hoping there would be a job in the Brooklyn Dodgers organization—doing anything. One day he read in the classifieds that the Hopkinsville Hoppers in rural Kentucky were holding open tryouts. He knew the opportunity to play at the professional level—even just in class D ball in the Kitty League—had to pay more than the $80 a month he was making at Heshie's. Plus, this was a chance to live out a dream. He packed the black metal spikes he wore at Tilden along with his two baseball gloves and bought a one-way ticket for a bus he thought would take him to baseball heaven.

A JEW FROM Brooklyn in a pastoral Kentucky town during the early 1950s . . . pretty unusual. But so was my dad.

Upon his arrival, he half-jokingly nicknamed himself the Duke of Hopkinsville after his hero from back home. He showed up along with about thirty-five other hopefuls and was put through a series of skill-assessment tests. He wanted to pitch, so he was asked to throw twenty-five fastballs and twenty-five curveballs under the watchful eye of the minor league coaches. Dad made the team as a pitcher/first baseman. He was thrilled to be making $200 a month while keeping his dream of playing for the Dodgers alive.

The level of competition was noticeably higher than back in Brooklyn, but that wasn't the problem. The bigger issue was that many of his teammates had never met a Jew before, and despite his attempts to be funny and friendly, he was ostracized from the first day. Now he knew how Jackie Robinson felt. He stayed on for several weeks, pitching a little and playing some first base, but soon he couldn't take it anymore. The clincher was when a hometown fan, seated close to the field, taunted him while he was playing first base: "Hey, Jew boy, where are your horns?" The hate-filled remarks spread like a cancer through the first few rows behind him. Dozens of fans added cruel gibes. After that, Dad just wanted to get the hell out of Hopkinsville. He felt hated and alone.

Back in Brooklyn, he took a series of odd jobs while looking for a career to settle into. That's how he found himself in Manhattan, heading to an interview for a shipping clerk's position, on October 3, 1951—the day that broke Dodgers fans' hearts.

Of course, the Dodgers would break his heart all over again

Dad pitches the opening-day game for the U.S. Army Special Forces team in Germany, 1954. *From the author's collection*

six years later, when they moved to Los Angeles. Jack was a real working-class man with the pride and determination that defined Brooklyn in the postwar era. When his beloved Dodgers left in 1957, he was as angry and resentful as anyone. These were *his* Dodgers, and they were leaving home, never to return. To this day, he doesn't like to talk much about it.

Still, Dad never lost his love of baseball. Even as he worked as a beverage deliveryman, carrying thirty-five-pound cases of soda, beer, and seltzer up three or four flights of stairs, he kept playing ball in pickup games on the fields at Brooklyn's Prospect Park Parade Grounds, the same baseball diamonds where many local legends have played before and since: Sandy Koufax, Joe Torre, Willie Randolph, and Manny Ramirez among them. Getting drafted into the U.S. Army and being sent to Germany during the Korean War didn't stop him from playing either. He joined the Special Forces team, where one of his teammates was a tall right-handed hurler named Johnny Kucks, who would go on to pitch for the Yankees—and shut out the Dodgers in game 7 of the 1956 World

Series. After Dad was honorably discharged from the Army, he gave up on his own baseball dreams, but he kept rooting for the Dodgers—even after they fled Brooklyn.

As upset as he was about the Dodgers' leaving, he stayed a Dodger fan because of one player—another Jewish lefty from Brooklyn, Sandy Koufax. Dad had a strong affinity for Koufax. They were close in age and came from the same Brooklyn community. In 1965, Dad's hero set off a firestorm of controversy when he refused to pitch game 1 of the World Series against the Minnesota Twins because it fell on the holiest day of the Jewish calendar, Yom Kippur. Koufax was chastised by hordes of media members and fans. Dad felt for Koufax, his Hopkinsville experience still fresh in his mind all those years later.

By that point, Dad had met my mom—a Brooklynite like him—and gotten married. They would have three kids: Steve, Rebecca, and me. Eventually Mom and Dad would, like the Dodgers before them, move out of Brooklyn. In my parents' case, they went to nearby Howard Beach, a neighborhood in Queens sandwiched between Brooklyn and Long Island. They bought a two-family house—what was then called a mother/daughter house—and our grandparents lived upstairs, with the rest of the family taking the main floor and basement.

Our family was still living in that same Howard Beach house decades later when my dad, by then managing eight Salvation Army thrift stores on Long Island, made a fateful discovery. In the early spring of 1990, while making his usual rounds, he stopped in at the store in Levittown just as one of the Salvation Army trucks pulled up with a fresh delivery of merchandise. The workers unloaded old picture frames, tattered furniture, used clothing, glassware, a bedroom set, and an armchair. Among this typical assortment of no-longer-wanted possessions, my dad noticed a large cardboard box filled with bric-a-brac. Sitting atop was a vintage-looking baseball. The old ballplayer was intrigued. His eyes followed the ball as it made its way inside the store.

The store manager, a woman named Thea Wudyka, started to plot out where she was going to display the new items. My dad asked her about the baseball. Barely giving it a moment's thought, she told him that she'd probably just put it on a low shelf and maybe some kid would buy it for a few bucks.

Dad asked to take a look. Something about it caught his eye. It was honey-colored, suggesting that it had been around for a long time and that maybe it had even been used in a game. It had the look and feel of a pro ball, with its tight, wide red stitching. Dad studied it carefully and was shocked by what he discovered. Clearly visible on the ball were names, big names: Willie Mays, Bobby Thomson, Sal Maglie, Hank Schenz, Leo Durocher, Wes Westrum, Alvin Dark, Larry Jansen, Hank Thompson, Bill Rigney, Don Mueller—practically the entire New York Giants roster from 1951.

My dad was no fan of the Giants, of course. But in forty years, those white-hot feelings of hatred he had experienced on the sidewalk in front of that Manhattan bar had mellowed. These were the signatures of guys he had watched and followed, some all-stars and even Hall of Famers who had given him years' worth of entertainment. It did not even occur to him at the time that the ball might be the one that Thomson had hit out of the Polo Grounds. But he thought it would make a fun souvenir—a cool relic from baseball's glory days as well as his own.

He offered Mrs. Wudyka two bucks for the ball, and she accepted. When he took the ball home he placed it on top of his armoire.

My dad's armoire was a legendary piece of furniture in our family. It was solid wood, nearly six feet tall and at least four feet wide, and so sturdy that it was almost immovable. Dad used the top of it in lieu of a traditional filing system. He would toss everything up there: old receipts, ticket stubs, mail, hats, medication bottles, an oversize penny jar shaped like Snoopy. My mom was always on him to clean off that armoire but somehow he avoided the daunting task. The ball was soon swallowed up by all of Dad's other junk. There it sat for years, apparently forgotten.

The Armoire

Wednesday, October 3, 1951

Sandy Zucker grew up on Vermont Street near the border of Brownsville and East New York, and she loved the Dodgers. Her most prized possession was an autograph book of Dodger signatures, everyone from catcher Roy Campanella to pitcher Clem Labine to shortstop Pee Wee Reese. She was a huge fan of the "Little Colonel," as Reese was known, because of his grittiness and leadership.

She and a few friends were supposed to watch the deciding game together over at Sydelle Saltman's house on New Lots Avenue. The Saltmans were the first family on the block to have a TV. But Sandy's parents wouldn't let her skip a day at Jefferson High. To make matters worse, she had a bookkeeping job that began right after school at 4:00 p.m. That should have meant she'd miss the end of the game too, but her boss knew all about her passion for the Dodgers and was willing to give her the afternoon off. So she figured she'd be out of school and at Sydelle's in time to watch the Dodgers celebrate—or so she hoped.

Sandy, like thousands of other New York kids stuck in school that day, needed to come up with a scheme for following the game during class. Fortunately for her, her friend Barbara Vidor had such a plan. Right before their history class, Barbara told the assistant principal that she had to make an emergency phone call home—a matter of life or death. But really, the call was to her father, who gleefully informed

Sandy Zucker (Mom) in 1953, on her stoop, Vermont Street, Brooklyn.
From the author's collection

her that the Dodgers were leading 4-1. He cautioned her, though, that Don Newcombe, Brooklyn's pitcher, was wearing down.

For the rest of the school day, the girls counted down the seconds until dismissal.
At the sound of the bell, they bolted out the front doors of the school's Pennsylvania
Avenue exit and ran thirteen blocks to Sydelle's house, sure they were about to join
a Dodger celebration. Instead, Sydelle's TV showed the ninth inning in progress
and the Giants just moments away from crushing hearts all over Brooklyn. The
sharp-sounding crack of Thomson's bat made the girls' hearts sink just as fast as the
line drive. Sandy's beloved Dodgers would have to wait till next year, as the famous
Dodger rallying cry went . . . again.

Sandy and Barbara barely had a chance to speak a word to Sydelle before the home run, and they certainly couldn't find anything to say after it. They filed out of her house and onto the silent streets of Brooklyn, dazed and dejected.

I SUPPOSE I never really had a choice but to become a baseball fanatic. My dad was not the only one in the house who felt the game in his blood. My mother, too, was a big fan. She was just as passionate about the Dodgers as Dad was. When I was a kid, we talked about baseball all the time. She'd recite the lineup of the '55 Dodgers for me. Gilliam, Reese, Snider, Hodges, Campanella, and so on. She spoke those hallowed names like a prayer, with deep pride and a twinkle in her speckled green eyes.

I also remember her telling me that her single biggest regret in life was that when she moved from Brownsville to Flatbush to live with my dad, she didn't take her book of Dodger autographs with her. When she went to look for it later, she found that her parents, not big baseball fans, had thrown it in the garbage. She must have told me that story a dozen times.

In fact, it was the Dodgers who helped bring my parents together. They met on a blind date at the Barge restaurant in Sheepshead Bay shortly after the Dodgers had left Brooklyn in 1957. They hit it off right away, bonding over the shared loss of their beloved team. Many of their early conversations were about the Dodgers. They talked about not just the sense of betrayal they felt, but also the vivid memories "Dem Bums" had provided. There were the crushing losses, sure—including, of course, the vicious blow that Bobby Thomson had landed in 1951. But there were high points as well. No moment was sweeter than October 4, 1955, when the Dodgers won their first ever World Series. Dad remembered sitting in a booth with three buddies at St. John's Bar, on Utica Avenue and St. John's Place, screaming at the TV as they watched Johnny Podres pitch one for the

Sandy Zucker (Mom), summer of
1954 in Nantucket, Massachusetts.
From the author's collection

ages—a complete game shutout to beat the Yankees 2-0 and bring the
long-awaited championship to where it belonged—Brooklyn.

During their courtship and the early years of their marriage,
Mom and Dad didn't have a team to root for. Sure, Dad kept following the Dodgers, but that was only because of his man Koufax.
So it was something of a relief when New York welcomed a National League expansion team in 1962: the Mets, whose colors hon-
ored the two teams that had departed the city after 1957—blue for
the Dodgers and orange for the Giants.

Mom and Dad adopted the Mets as their team almost immediately, and Dad finally gave up his tenuous attachment to the Dodgers. My mom would be a committed fan for decades, until the 1994
baseball strike, which disappointed her so much that she vowed
never to watch another major league game. She kept her promise

for a few years but softened when McGwire and Sosa were competing for the single-season home-run mark in 1998. She was hooked again.

WITH BOTH OF my parents rooting for the Mets, naturally I became a devoted fan of the team also. In grade school, my bedroom was right next to the bathroom my dad would use to get ready for work every morning. I would wake up to the sound of his listening to 1010 WINS radio while shaving. If he'd gone to bed before the end of the previous night's Mets game, he would turn up the volume as soon as the sports report came on, to hear the result. I couldn't hear the radio clearly but I could tell by his reaction whether they'd won or lost.

By the time I became a teenager, I was confident and good with people, but I was more interested in girls than school. I was uninspired by my classes and had no idea what I wanted to do with my life. But throughout my upbringing, baseball and family were two constants.

Dad and I bonded over the Mets throughout my childhood. We were big football fans too (every Sunday in the fall we'd head to Bayside, Queens, to watch the NFL games with my cousin Marlon, a bookie who had installed a giant satellite dish—one of the first made for home use—on his parents' roof), but our true sports year started with the Mets' spring training. Even though we never managed to fly down to Florida to see them in person, watching the young hopefuls on channel 9 was an annual rite of spring. Dad and I would each play scout, trying to predict which prospects would make the opening-day roster. Our scouting acumen wasn't exactly bulletproof. I remember being convinced that 1984's number one draft pick was going to be the man to lead the Mets to the promised land. It wasn't Dwight Gooden or Darryl Strawberry who caught my eye, but a lanky outfielder named Shawn Abner. He never made it with the Mets and was gone in a trade a few years later; he ended up hitting only .227 for his major league career.

Dad and I went to a lot of Mets games at Shea Stadium, especially the Saturday matinees. And together we watched every game of the World Series champion '86 Mets when I was nineteen years old. Growing up in Howard Beach, I felt a constant pull toward trouble. It was Mafia king John Gotti's neighborhood, and he was idolized by most of my friends. Sensing I was heading into dangerous waters, my dad used sports to distract me. We spent so much time together watching and attending sporting events that we eventually became inseparable best friends, particularly when it came to baseball. Game 6 of that World Series against the Boston Red Sox (now remembered simply as the Bill Buckner game) is one of the most famous in baseball history, but game 6 of the National League Championship Series was just as memorable for us.

That game fell on a Wednesday afternoon in October, just like the Thomson game. The Mets were in Houston taking on the Astros and needed one more win to clinch the pennant. The pressure was on because the Mets desperately wanted to avoid facing Houston's seemingly unhittable ace, Mike Scott, in a possible Game 7. My whole family watched the game in the den of our Howard Beach house. We were all Mets fans except for my big brother, Steve, a Yankees fan who was obnoxiously rooting for the Astros.

It was a back-and-forth game—a sixteen-inning epic—and my sister's fiancé, Mitch, called on the phone after each big moment. We could hear him screaming through the earpiece of the phone

Me and Dad in 1986, the New York Mets' championship season. *From the author's collection*

even though it was mounted on the wall in the kitchen, fifteen feet from the den.

In the top of the fourteenth inning, Mets second baseman Wally Backman singled home Darryl Strawberry to give the Mets a 4-3 lead. Things were looking good. But the Astros' Billy Hatcher homered to tie the game in the bottom half of the inning, and Steve went crazy, laughing in our pained faces.

That's when my dad took me aside. He and I had been together through this entire season, and he wouldn't let his oldest son ruin what the Mets had been building. Dad told me that Steve was a jinx and we had to get away from him. To change our luck, he and I went down to the basement to watch the rest of the game on a thirteen-inch black-and-white TV set. The reception was lousy, so Dad fashioned a coat-hanger antenna. We lit a candle and placed it on top of the TV to bless the room and ward off Steve's bad mojo from upstairs. The plan worked. The Mets scored three runs in the top of the sixteenth inning to go ahead for good and advance to the World Series.

I hadn't been alive for the Thomson game, but I knew enough from my parents to understand that no fan would want to endure an ending anywhere near as painful. Like most sports fans, I'm superstitious, and I'll always be grateful to my dad for rescuing us—and the Mets—from such an agonizing fate.

MY PASSION FOR the Mets remained undiminished, but so did my distaste for formal education. I headed off to college but, bored by my classes, I ended up bouncing around a few different schools.

I finally finished at Queens Borough College in 1989, attending night classes while working during the day as a cub reporter at *Sportstyle* magazine, a sports business publication and division of Fairchild Publications. I was promoted to assistant editor and immediately knew I was cut out to work in sports journalism. I interviewed athletes, including flashy two-sport star Deion Sanders, New York Knicks great Patrick Ewing, and Dodgers Cy Young Award winner Orel Hershiser (who had dominated the Mets in the 1988 playoffs). But it was an interview I did with Mickey Mantle that proved to be the highlight—not least because it so impressed my dad.

Throughout the 1950s, New York baseball was headlined by three men who patrolled center field: Willie Mays, Mickey Mantle, and Duke Snider. Debates about which one was the best were like background music in the barrooms of the city. The Duke was always my dad's favorite, of course. And Mays, the legend who ended his career with the Mets, held a special appeal for me. But somehow

Mantle, with his three MVPs and seven World Series titles, captured my imagination the most. Even though he was a Yankee, I
was in awe of him.

I got to meet the Mick in 1991. He had opened a restaurant in Manhattan a few years earlier, and Nike was using his
memorabilia-filled dining room as the site of a press conference
announcing a new line of sneakers and apparel for the 1992 U.S.
Olympic basketball squad, which had been dubbed the Dream Team.
The event was emblematic of two big trends in sports—the growing
memorabilia market that had made everything from trading cards
to game-used equipment increasingly valuable, and the even more
recent craze for athlete-endorsed sportswear, especially shoes. Ever
since the explosion of Nike's Air Jordans, the sporting goods companies had been churning out sneaker lines peddled by famous athletes. I was at Mickey Mantle's to cover the launch of the Air Force
180, which Charles Barkley would make famous by wearing in the
games in Barcelona.

While the crowd was focused on the presentation, which included appearances by Dream Teamers Patrick Ewing and Chris
Mullen, I edged over to where Mantle was standing. Like many old
ballplayers, he looked prematurely aged, his face full of wrinkles
from spending so many afternoons in the sun. He was wearing a
black mock turtleneck with a blue blazer and tan slacks. Even from
across the room, I could see that his hands were large, coarse, and
beaten up, like a construction worker's. He had all his hair, but it
looked colored, except for the graying on the sides. Interviewing
him was not part of my actual assignment, but I couldn't resist.

I waited for Mantle to finish a conversation he was having with a
PR guy and quickly made my move. Just as he turned to walk away,
I reached out my hand and introduced myself. He looked surprised
that I didn't want to talk about his new upscale restaurant or the

Nike press conference, and he gladly relived his glory years with me for a short while. I asked him about some of the best pitchers he'd ever faced. He quickly mentioned Warren Spahn and Sandy Koufax. Of course I pressed him on Koufax, thinking how fantastic it would be to tell my dad what the Mick said. He brought up the 1963 season, in which Koufax beat his Yankees twice in the World Series. "Koufax had as good a stuff as I had ever seen, and I didn't even have to try to hit him left-handed," said Mantle, who was a switch hitter.

My father had been proud when I landed a job as a journalist, but after I told him I'd met the Mick face-to-face, he had a new-found admiration for my work. As I recounted my conversation with Mantle to him word for word, Dad admitted that even though Duke Snider was his favorite player, Mantle's combination of speed and power made him the best player he ever saw.

As a sports journalist, I often covered memorabilia events and shows, including the SGMA Team Sports Show, the annual Super Show in Atlanta, as well as various product launches from companies ranging from Steiner Sports Marketing to Upper Deck. Through the 1990s, the market continued its ascent into the mainstream. It had gone from being an obscure hobby to a billion-dollar-a-year business. Trading cards were particularly popular. In 1991, hockey superstar Wayne Gretzky partnered with the L.A. Kings team owner, Bruce McNall, to purchase one of the famous Honus Wagner T-206 baseball cards for $451,000. The 1952 Topps Mickey Mantle card was routinely selling for $200,000. Men all over the country were lamenting the day their moms threw away their old baseball cards.

But cards were just the beginning. Around this time, the controversial NBA star Dennis Rodman became famous for taking off his jerseys and throwing them into the stands. This began a boom in game-used jerseys that extended to all the other major sports. Game-used baseballs also found their way into the sports-crazed psyche of collectors. In 1992, actor Charlie Sheen paid $93,500 for the ball New York Mets outfielder Mookie Wilson hit through the legs of Boston's Bill Buckner during game 6 of the 1986 World Series. Auction houses everywhere were cashing in.

In the midst of this memorabilia fever, I left my writing job to pursue new opportunities in the world of film. I started film school at Hunter College and also began work on a screenplay about two adventurous young men traveling across America on Amtrak, trying to see if they could make it with less than $500 between them. The story was based on actual events. My old pal Alex Carone ("Crazy Al") and I actually accomplished this feat years earlier, leaving from Penn Station and eventually making it to my close friend Bob Makela's place in Los Angeles, unannounced. The screenplay was the first I had ever written and it won honorable mention in the American Screenwriters Association competition. I knew then that I wanted to continue writing nonfiction and making films. Besides sports, my other favorite pastime had always been movies, and I was already trying to think of a way to combine my passions.

After film school, I got another job, writing and producing on-air promotions for ABC; started doing freelance work at USA Network; and even wrote and produced an off-Broadway play. Financially secure and gaining traction in my chosen industry, I became engaged to my South American girlfriend, Jolis, who had come to the United States a few years earlier to work as a nanny for a family in Oyster Bay, Long Island. I bought an apartment off Fifth Avenue overlooking Central Park. Here I was, a kid from Queens living on the Upper East Side of Manhattan. I'd come a long way from Howard Beach.

But for me, the good times didn't last. In 2000, my dream life quickly turned into a nightmare. First I was diagnosed with a rare, painful bladder disease called interstitial cystitis, which forced me to leave my job. This put tremendous strain on my marriage, which ended in a long, torturous divorce in 2004. My anger at my wife eventually turned inward and morphed into crippling depression. This despair was punctuated by panic attacks that kept me from leaving the house. I was forced to sell the place that I had once been so proud of and move back in with my parents, into the two-family home I had grown up in as a kid.

Each morning I awoke trembling. Fear and anxiety, mixed with severe depression, made each day a struggle to survive. My mom would come to the bedroom, gently take my hand, and tell me, "You are going to get through this. Even if I have to sit here all day with you and take it five minutes at a time. Take deep breaths. You will get better. Your father and I won't give up until you do."

Dad was usually in the kitchen making toast for me. It was all I could keep down. By eight A.M., I was vomiting from nerves—the first of many times in a usual day. I pretty much did not leave their house for a six-month stretch. Dad had to walk my dog for me. Only visits to the psychiatric unit at Long Island Jewish Hospital could get me outside. Dad drove me because I was too heavily medicated to drive myself.

ONE DAY IN the late spring of 2004 during the deepest part of my depression, my dad was browsing through the magazine section in a Barnes & Noble not far from home. Just as he had religiously checked the *Sporting News* as a young man, he still made a point to read everything about sports that he could. He finished looking at *Sports Illustrated* and picked up *Beckett's Sports Collectibles Magazine*.

Inside he saw a full-page advertisement that immediately grabbed his attention. The headline read: LELAND'S GUARANTEES $1 MILLION FOR THOMSON BALL.

Bells went off in Dad's head. The ad, placed by Lelands Sports Auctions on Long Island, went on to detail how Thomson's home-run ball—the Shot Heard 'Round the World—had never been found. Josh Evans, the owner of Lelands, was offering a million-dollar reward for anyone who could somehow prove to have the long-sought prize. My dad's mind raced. What if that baseball he had paid two bucks for fourteen years earlier—the one with all the signatures of the '51 Giants—was worth a million dollars? What if the guy who caught it had never realized its monetary value but had held on to the souvenir through the years? Perhaps he had moved to the suburbs and then, after he passed away, his wife unknowingly donated it to the thrift store along with a shag rug and a Joe DiMaggio Mr. Coffee pot. Not impossible. And for a million bucks, it was certainly worth finding out, or trying to.

So Dad rushed home from the bookstore. But there was one problem: He couldn't find the baseball. From my bed, I heard him frantically searching around. After so many years of not paying attention to the ball, he had no idea where it was. He thought he had left it on top of his armoire, but it wasn't there. He turned the house upside down, looking in the top of his closet, under his bed, in boxes in the basement. He drove my mother crazy asking her to help him look for it. But he came away empty handed.

After a month, he gave up. He resigned himself to the fact that the ball, as well as the million dollars, was gone.

But there was one place they hadn't checked.

In the second week of July, by some small miracle of fate, Mom arranged to have the inside of the house painted. I was having one of my good days—which meant I was able to get out of bed and leave my room. I was standing with my dad in his bedroom when the painters asked his permission to move his armoire into the center of the room. The two of us looked on as they lifted the massive piece of furniture and pulled it away from the wall. As they did, we heard something thump against the hardwood floor and then watched as the long-missing thrift-store baseball, in all its beat-up glory, bounced out from underneath the armoire and rolled between Dad's feet.

The baseball Dad purchased for $2 at the Salvation Army Thrift Shop in 1990, Ford Frick stamp and all.
Photograph by Matthew Klein

THREE

Dad vs. Lelands

At some point over the years, it turns out, my father's potential million-dollar ticket had rolled backward off the armoire and become lodged against the wall. And now, amazingly, it had come free and was back in my dad's hands.

Having spent weeks searching fruitlessly for the ball, Dad sprung into action. That afternoon he called Lelands and set up a meeting with owner Josh Evans, who had placed the ad. Lelands was gearing up for its biannual sports auction and trying to attract as much attention as possible by offering a million dollars for the Thomson ball. Even though the auction would be held a year later, the Thomson ball was unquestionably the biggest draw, so Evans wasted no time in getting the word out. Lelands already did brisk business. It had been ten years since I had first noticed the boom in the memorabilia market, and things had only gotten crazier. The ball that Mark McGwire hit for his 70th home run in 1998 sold for $3 million. Auction houses such as Lelands had a vested interest in finding the biggest-ticket sports memorabilia items as a way to earn large commissions.

With so much at stake, Dad grew a little nervous about the meeting. To put himself more at ease, he prepared for his appointment at Lelands by doing some research. He learned that a 1951 baseball would have a Spalding logo on it. He was relieved to find one on his ball, clearly visible, sandwiched between the signatures of Sal Maglie and Don Mueller.

But the advertisement included one detail that concerned him. It stated that the Thomson ball would feature the stamped signature of National League president Warren Giles. Dad's ball had a stamped signature all right, but it read Ford Frick, not Warren Giles. A little worried about this, Dad decided to call the National Baseball Hall of Fame in Cooperstown, New York. He eventually reached museum curator Ted Spencer, who explained the source of the confusion. Back in the fifties, official American League and National League baseballs had the names of the league presidents stamped on them. Ford Frick was in fact the National League president at the start of 1951. In late September, just before the end of the regular season, he was promoted to commissioner of baseball, and several days later, Warren Giles was named to succeed Frick as National League president. Significantly, Giles's appointment did not become effective until *after* the 1951 season ended. More to the point, because Giles was announced as the successor so late in the 1951 season, the National League baseballs used in the remaining games that year still bore Frick's signature.

Dad researched the subject independently and corroborated Spencer's account. He went back to the Barnes & Noble and flipped through several sports fact books and came across *The Sports Encyclopedia: Baseball* by David S. Neft, Richard M. Cohen, and Michael L. Neft, which confirmed Ford Frick's position as National League president. He figured that Lelands was confused about the Frick/

Giles changeover. Armed with his research, Dad was confident that he could explain the situation and still be in the running for the million dollars.

THE LELANDS STORE was located in Seaford, on the south shore of Long Island, about an hour's drive from my dad's place in Howard Beach. On the day of his meeting, Dad arrived to find a storefront that wasn't much to look at from the outside: It was small, made of red brick, and had nothing in the window. Above the door was a big sign that read LELANDS in white script on a red background.

Inside, the office space wasn't much more impressive. It felt industrial, like a warehouse. There was a section with cubicles and a few windowless private offices. My dad couldn't see the actual merchandise—it was in the back room and down in the basement. But the long, narrow hallway leading to the waiting room was covered with framed autographed pictures of Sparky Lyle, Joe Frazier, and other famous athletes.

A few minutes after my dad entered the waiting room, a slim man with dark hair and a goatee approached. Looking more like a stockbroker in his suit and tie than a sports collectables dealer, he introduced himself as the president of Lelands, Mike Heffner. "Josh will be in to join us in a minute," Heffner said. "Are you a collector, Mr. Biegel?"

"I have a few things, but I wouldn't call myself a collector."

Shortly after, Josh Evans himself walked in. He was bald, overweight, and dressed very casually. He seemed more withdrawn and subdued than his colleague, keeping his distance and greeting my father with a brief nod. He said, "So, Mike tells me that you think you have the Thomson ball. Can I see it?"

Dad reached into his black canvas attaché and pulled out the ball with great care, as if it were a Fabergé egg. Evans took the ball and glanced at it quickly.

"I see there are lots of autographs. Did you get them yourself?"

"They were on the ball when I bought it fourteen years ago."

Evans turned the ball at angles and held it to the light. "Well," he said finally, "that's definitely Willie Mays's signature."

Dad was starting to get excited. "I've had the ball all this time. I had no idea until I read your ad that it might be the Thomson ball."

Heffner had smiled when Evans authenticated the Mays signature. "It does look very old," he said optimistically. "Josh, what do you think?"

Then, as Dad had feared, Evans brought up the stamp issue. "I see one glaring problem. It's got the wrong league president, so I don't know—"

Dad was prepared with his response and he jumped right in: "Actually, I noticed the ad said that Warren Giles's name should be on the ball. I believe that's a mistake."

Evans was clearly not used to having people question him, and he became visibly agitated. "Mr. Biegel, that's no mistake. I've been working in this business for over twenty years."

Undaunted, Dad continued: "No disrespect to you, but I spoke to the Baseball Hall of Fame and they agreed that Ford Frick should be on the baseball. I also researched it in a sports history book—"

Evans, losing his patience, cut Dad off. "The Baseball Hall of Fame? They make mistakes all the time. They have balls in there that are supposed to be signed by Babe Ruth that were really signed by his wife. They don't know the difference. *I* do. *They* are not experts in this field."

Evans's extreme reaction aggravated my dad. He decided to try again. "But it's also in books that it should be Frick's name. Believe me, I didn't come here to waste your time. I did my homework. How can you say it should be Giles's name on the ball when all the evidence says it should say Frick?"

"Because I'm a curator. I can tell you what year a ball was from by looking at the dirt on it."

The absurdity of that last statement really struck Dad. Now he lost it.

"What kind of show are you guys running? What makes you a curator anyway? It's not like there's some special advanced degree for authenticating dirt."

Heffner, who seemed to genuinely want to avoid this conflict, stepped in. "Sorry, Mr. Biegel. But Josh is the expert. I know you're disappointed. But this is our field. We can authenticate the signatures but not the ball."

When Dad had first approached Lelands, he wasn't sure he had the Thomson ball. But it made him furious that Evans had no idea what he was talking about or at least was too stubborn to acknowledge that he might have made an error. After his encounter with Evans, Dad became more and more convinced that his ball was *the* ball. He now knew the signatures were real. And he was soon to discover for certain that the ball was definitely from the 1951 season. How did he know this? Because Hank Schenz's name was on the ball. Schenz joined the Giants just twelve weeks before the playoff series and was gone by 1952. So the ball *had* to be from approximately the same time as the big game. Also, for the whole team to sign a ball, he reasoned, it must be a very special object. I later learned that signed baseballs were fairly common, but he didn't know that, and probably wouldn't have cared if he did. Rationally or not, he now believed in his heart that he had the ball and nothing was going to convince him otherwise.

WHEN DAD ARRIVED home later that evening, I overheard him telling my mom what had happened. Still enraged the next day, he came to me. He knew that I could be a tenacious ally, and he wanted to call on me in particular because of my experience as a reporter digging up information. But he also knew this was a delicate situation, given how broken I was. Dad explained what had gone on at Lelands and asked whether I could do some research on Evans, the self-appointed guru.

Even though I was living in a constant state of fear, anxiety, and depression, the urgency in my dad's voice made me want to help. At the very least, I thought, I could do some Internet research on Lelands and Josh Evans. I promised him several days in a row, "This will be the day, Poppa." Days turned into weeks until I finally admitted to him I was not well enough to assist. Clinical depression rendered me mentally powerless, and massive anxiety attacks required heavy sedation. I suggested he ask my brother or someone else—anyone else—as I was simply incapable at the time. Dad understood and told me to just try to focus on getting well; this fight was not over, and I'd have another opportunity to stand by his side.

Dad's next move was to contact a lawyer named Larry Rosen, a family friend. He explained what had happened. Rosen researched the Frick/Giles discrepancy and found old newspaper accounts from when Giles took office as National League president—*after* the 1951 season—on November 1, 1951. He sent a letter with the supporting documents to Lelands and requested that Evans make a retraction of the ad in the next edition of *Beckett's,* explaining how Lelands had made an error about the Giles stamp, and offer a written apology to Dad. Even if Lelands wasn't going to sell Jack's ball, having that ad on record listing its inaccurate criteria might keep *anyone* from purchasing his ball. Evans did not respond to several calls and letters from Rosen. After months of not hearing back from Lelands, Rosen suggested that Dad wait until the spring 2005 auction grew closer before making another move.

During that time, I slowly began climbing out of the darkness, largely because of the unconditional support I felt from my mom and dad. It began fueling my desire to regain a sense of self. And all those months later, I still had Dad's standing offer for me to help him prove his ball was the original Shot Heard 'Round the World, even if it meant discrediting Lelands. Now I was ready to give it another try. The June auction was just a few months away, and my brain was functioning well enough to help my dad.

I started researching Lelands Auction House, and the first red flag that popped up was when I read an article in the *New York Post* about how the family of Hall of Fame outfielder Roberto Clemente was planning a lawsuit against Lelands. Clemente had been tragically killed in a plane crash on New Year's Eve 1972 while trying to transport relief supplies to earthquake victims in Nicaragua. Evans and company had been set to auction off two pieces of the DC-7 plane. The Clemente family was understandably outraged, and Lelands was lambasted in the press for its tastelessness. Only after legal action was threatened and the bad publicity ensued did Lelands pull the item from auction.

Meanwhile, with the auction less than a month away, much to our surprise, Dad received a call from Michael Heffner. The local CBS news affiliate was coming to the store, Heffner said, to do a story on a few of the guys in the running to collect the reward. He asked if Dad would like to be a part of the piece.

"Does this mean you guys finally did some research and discovered that I'm right about the stamp on the ball?"

Heffner replied, "We'll talk about that when you get down here."

Dad agreed to go. Now his mind ran off in many directions. He did not trust Lelands after hearing the Clemente plane story and after his own experience there. But part of him figured that at the very least this would give him another chance to confront Evans—and on TV, no less. And an even bigger part of him thought Evans and Heffner might have come to their senses. After all, the historical records clearly indicated that Dad was right about the signature. And the more he thought about it, the more excited he got. So he took his car to the Crossbay Car Wash for a wax and cleaning, visited the barber for a fresh haircut, and bought a new button-down shirt from the Gap. Dad was going back to Lelands in style. This time, he'd convince them he had the real ball.

WE DON'T KNOW how many people contacted Lelands saying they might have the Thomson ball, but we're sure there were at least three: my dad, Steve Fader, and Bill Moore.

Fader was about fifty-five years old, a thin guy, roughly five eight, with red hair and freckles. His eyes darted around while he talked, and his tone was uncertain and nervous. He told me that Giants manager Leo Durocher ended up with the ball after the game and that Durocher was a regular customer of Fader's uncle Gus, who owned a dry-cleaning store on Houston Street in Manhattan. Fader claimed that Durocher gave Gus the ball. This story struck me as nearly impossible to believe. How would Durocher end up with the ball at all? And if he did, why wouldn't he have given it to Thomson? Why would he have given it to his dry cleaner, of all people?

In another version, Fader told me that his uncle Gus was at the game, sitting in the left-field stands. When the ball cleared the wall, it landed on the stadium floor and Gus grabbed it from the bottom of the scrum of eager fans. He later gave it to the five-year-old Steve Fader, telling him, "You hold on to this baseball. It might be worth something someday."

The Fader baseball, which had a greenish tint to it, featured some autographs, including that of Durocher himself. But there was no league president's stamp or anything else to suggest it was even game-used, let alone the Thomson ball. In fact, when I first held it in my hand, it felt lighter and looked smaller than a pro-size baseball.

Bill Moore was a few years older than Fader, an unassuming guy with a square face, light complexion, and thick, dark eyebrows. His baseball was, as the *Daily News* reported, "in dreadful shape." Neither a league president's stamp nor manufacturer's logo could be seen. Everything was worn away except some writing in blue ink: "1951 last game pennet [*sic*] won by NY B. Thompson [*sic*] home run last of 9th."

Moore claimed that a family friend whose name he couldn't remember gave the ball to his father a few days after the game. The man didn't have any children of his own and wanted a kid to treasure it forever. So he gave it to Moore's dad as a gift for little Bill. My dad's ball, of course, had no such romantic story attached to it. But he had more empirical evidence that his ball was the Thomson ball than Fader and Moore put together.

When Dad arrived at Lelands for the second time, he was ushered into that same waiting room. Sitting across from him was Bill Moore. Dad asked Moore if he could examine his ball. Moore happily obliged. Twisting and turning the ball under the fluorescent light, Dad wasn't too impressed. "Not much on here," he said. "Everything is washed away. All I see is some scribbled handwriting with a lot of misspelled words."

Moore shot back, "Well, it's enough for them to put it up for auction."

Dad was taken aback. "How do you know that?"

"They told me ten minutes ago. They even told the reporter."

Dad looked out the window of the waiting room, and there was Heffner being interviewed by Duke Castiglione of WCBS-TV. He pieced together what had happened: In an effort to get publicity for the upcoming auction, Lelands must have pitched a story to CBS about the hunt for the ball. For the piece they needed two talking heads, the "winner," Bill Moore, and the "loser," Jack Biegel. That's why Heffner had been so circumspect on the phone.

My dad was puzzled that Lelands could have chosen *any* ball as the possible Thomson ball, let alone one as generic as the Moore ball. He figured the next step would be to perform some sort of laboratory testing. Dad asked Moore how Lelands had come to choose his ball.

Moore replied, "They said it couldn't be 100 percent authenticated because of the condition it's in, but they're still going to auction it off. They say the ink on the ball is definitely from 1951, and they like the story about how I got it."

Dad asked whether Lelands had done any kind of formal testing on the ink. Moore just shook his head no. Apparently, Josh Evans could authenticate ink from 1951 the same way he claimed he could tell what year the dirt on an old ball was from—simply by looking at it. Dad didn't want to cause a scene. He thought the better approach would be to calmly explain his case to the reporter. He approached Castiglione.

"You're Duke Castiglione, right? I love your show. Were you named after Duke Snider?"

"People always ask me that, but I'm actually from Boston originally. You're Mr. Biegel, right? Sorry they didn't choose your baseball."

Heffner and Evans stood glaring at Dad as he made his case to Castiglione. "I feel like there is a terrible injustice being done. My baseball is more likely to be the ball than the one they're selling."

Dad set forth each piece of evidence—the Frick and Spalding stamps, Hank Schenz's name, the authenticated signatures—but in the end none of his story made the broadcast. The CBS news report that ran had only cutaway shots of my dad with Bill Moore sitting in the waiting room while Heffner talked about how Lelands might have found the lost treasure.

My dad was livid and started making phone calls. He thought it obvious that Lelands was more concerned with getting its commission than with getting the facts right. By this point, he had convinced himself that *his* ball was *the* Thomson ball. Dad must have called every newspaper on the East Coast to tell his side of the story. And he got some big names at sports desks to talk to him, including Vic Ziegel of the *Daily News* and Joe Gergen of *Newsday*. But no articles ran supporting his case. The message was clear: The New York media were interested in running stories about the Thomson ball. But they were going to need a lot more to go on than one man's hunch that he might have it.

Dad went so far as to plead his case directly to the protagonists of the drama themselves, Branca and Thomson. The two men appeared at an autograph signing at a mall on Long Island in the spring of 2005. Dad patiently waited in line for half an hour to show them the ball and explain that he thought it was the one Thomson hit out of the Polo Grounds fifty-four years earlier.

Dad (*standing*) with Ralph Branca and Bobby Thomson at an autograph show in 2005. *From the author's collection*

Dad's claims were rejected: Branca muttered under his breath and rolled his eyes. Thomson was kinder, but wasn't any more convinced.

A few weeks later, Lelands chose to officially auction off Moore's undistinguished baseball. It sold in the neighborhood of $50,000 to a private buyer. Moore didn't get the million because the ball couldn't be authenticated, but he did get his share of the purchase price. The *Daily News* ran an article about the sale of the "possible" Thomson ball. There was a brief, inglorious mention of how Jack Biegel, of Howard Beach, Queens, also thought he had the ball. My dad was angrier than ever.

Not wanting to leave any doubt on the signature question, I subsequently did my own research to confirm what Ted Spencer of the Hall of Fame, my father's digging, and Larry Rosen's investigation had revealed. Sure enough, I discovered several *New York Times* stories from 1951 that showed unequivocally that Ford Frick was still acting as National League president at the time of the Bobby Thomson game. On September 22, 1951, the *Times* reported that Ford Frick had been chosen commissioner of baseball but that he "said he would not abandon his National League post until the end of the fiscal year, Nov. 1, or until his successor as president has been selected." His successor was selected several days later. On September 27—less than a week before the Thomson game—the *Times* ran a story headlined NATIONAL LEAGUE FORMALLY OFFERS PRESIDENCY TO GILES OF THE REDS, though the piece noted that Warren Giles had not even accepted the offer yet.

Then, on October 3—just a matter of hours before Thomson smacked his famous home run—the *Times* reported on some notable figures who had been in attendance at the Polo Grounds the previous day: "Ford Frick, *doubling as president of the National League and Baseball Commissioner,* was in a box near the Giant dugout with Will Harridge, American League head, and Warren Giles, *who is to succeed Frick as boss of the National League soon*" (emphasis added).

Lelands never acknowledged its error to my dad.

WHEN LELANDS AUCTIONED off Bill Moore's baseball, Dad wanted to sue. He came into my room one afternoon while I was reading Eckhart Tolle's *Power of Now* and asked me whether I was up for helping him fight this battle. I had spent so many months grappling with my own problems that this was the first time in ages that I was able to reflect on and assist with someone else's. I urged him not to sue Lelands. I didn't want my dad to be that guy you read about in the papers filing a frivolous lawsuit.

In attendance at the Polo Grounds, October 2, 1951: (*left to right*) Will Harridge, American League president; Ford Frick, National League president; and Warren Giles, Cincinnati Reds general manager. *Courtesy of the New York* Daily News

He asked me what he should do instead. After thinking about the matter for a while, I told him that he should let me find the truth myself—I was a reporter, after all. Maybe I could prove that his ball was the Thomson ball. As I mouthed the words, I couldn't quite believe that I was undertaking this project. I still didn't feel ready to take care of myself, let alone help anyone else. But I wanted to find a way to thank him and my mom for all the unwavering support they'd shown me and maybe this was it.

I wasn't really sure at first that I'd be able to prove my dad's case, but I wanted to try. This was the first sign of life I had shown in nearly a year. That spark lit a fire: I *was* going to find out what really happened to Bobby Thomson's baseball. And by getting back out into the real world, I could give my parents the greatest gift of all—seeing their son happy again.

My career had been on hold for nearly twenty months. But that was about to change. As I thought about it over the next few days, I realized that this opportunity was a gift, a way for me to do what I'd wanted to do for so long—combine my love of sports and film. I spent the rest of that week writing a film proposal about the search for the Thomson ball. I still had plenty of contacts in the film world, as did my brother, who worked as a creative director in advertising. The initial response to my idea was enthusiastic.

But just because I'd made the decision to try to get on with my life didn't mean it would be easy. I got the news on a Monday that a production company was interested in the idea and wanted to have an in-person meeting that Friday. The rest of the week was a downward spiral. The only place I felt comfortable was in my room. And even there, I was so full of anxiety that my body was in revolt—I vomited at the thought of having to talk to someone who wasn't family. Driving myself into Manhattan for the meeting was out of the question. That's when my dad stepped in.

"I'll drive you," he told me, fixing me in his confident gaze. "If you need to throw up, throw up. You are going to do great in this meeting. This is what you're good at. This is what you do. Your mother and I have all the confidence in the world in you. You have to be strong, Brian."

And so we got in the car and headed into Manhattan. As we drove along the approach of the Fifty-ninth Street Bridge, nearing where I had made my home with my wife, I experienced flashbacks of the horrific experience of getting divorced from someone I had been with for eight years, and became consumed with how far I had fallen since. This should have been a glorious moment: a sit-down meeting with a production company that was clearly interested in my idea and ready to move forward with the project. The problem was, I wasn't sure I could even get out of the car. I was deliriously scared. I wasn't ready for this. What if I failed?

My dad saw the anxiety in my face. Having cared for me throughout my battle with depression and panic attacks, he knew what toxic thoughts were filling my head. He reminded me of what he had been saying to me for months: "The best revenge is success."

"You have to be strong, Brian," he told me once again. "You can do this. We're almost there. Just go into this meeting, tell them what you need to tell them. And then we'll go right back home."

He and my mom had always sacrificed for their three children. And now in my weakest moment, I wanted to summon up enough strength to make them proud. I remembered my first day at Little League in 1977. I was so nervous that I didn't want to take the field. But I knew my parents were watching from the stands, and that gave me confidence. I went out there and played—and hit a triple in my second at bat. And now I realized that my dad was right. I could do this.

We arrived at the building on West Twenty-seventh Street. I unwrapped a piece of spearmint gum, put it in my mouth, and looked over at Dad. Before he could say another word or make an encouraging gesture, I slipped my fingers around the metal door handle and threw the car door open. I had never been more motivated: I was going to find the truth about the Thomson ball for my dad—but also for myself.

Esther

By the fall of 2005, I had a desk and an assistant at Tangerine Films' offices in New York City. They shared space with Driver Media, a commercial production company, with whom they partnered to produce my film. The documentary was a go; now I had to figure out how in the world I was going to find out what happened to a ball that memorabilia collectors and countless others had spent decades hunting for, to no avail. Maybe my dad had it, maybe he didn't, but either way, my mission was to find the truth.

The first thing I needed to do, I realized, was to learn as much as I could about the 1951 deciding playoff game. As a sports fanatic, and more important, as the son of two die-hard Brooklyn Dodgers fans, I had long known about the strong sense of nostalgia that surrounded the game and Thomson's landmark home run. *Sports Illustrated* had voted it the second greatest sports moment of the twentieth century, behind only the 1980 U.S. Olympic hockey team's stunning upset of the mighty Soviet Union. But until I embarked on my research for this project, I hadn't realized what a seminal moment it truly was.

Bobby Thomson graciously thanks the piece of lumber he used to smack the game-winning home run, defeating the rival Brooklyn Dodgers on October 3, 1951. *Courtesy of the National Baseball Hall of Fame Library, Cooperstown, NY*

For starters, I came to understand that the enduring significance of the event didn't simply reflect parochialism on the part of New York baseball fans. It was, in fact, no coincidence that this landmark moment featured two teams from New York City, which was by far the biggest baseball town in America at the time. Three of major league baseball's sixteen teams played in the city then. It was a fascinating era in New York sports, as each team had a unique character: the Yankees, dominant and professional, who won almost every year; the Giants, a team of faded glory who had struggled during and just after World War II but seemed poised to regain prominence with the arrival of their young star, Willie Mays; and the Dodgers, the perennial underdogs, who were hopeless for decades before a solid two seasons in 1940 and 1941, then began a great run with the arrival of Jackie Robinson in 1947. The Dodgers defined working-class Brooklyn and had as strong a bond with their fans as any team in pro sports.

The classic 1951 three-game playoff series between the Giants and the Dodgers was the pinnacle of these glory days of New York baseball. It shared the front page of the *New York Times* with a credible story about a possible nuclear attack by the Soviets—such was the level of its importance. And the result affected the entire country, not just New York. Thomson's home run was the golden moment in what has come to be called the golden age of baseball—the era when the major leagues had finally been integrated, meaning that baseball fans could now see the most talented ballplayers in the world compete against one another. The shocking result of the final game was front-page news from coast to coast. Legendary sportswriter Red Smith, whose *New York Herald Tribune* column was syndicated in ninety newspapers across the country, wrote this after the game: "Now it is done. Now the story ends. And there is no way to tell it. The art of fiction is dead. Reality has strangled invention. Only the utterly impossible, the inexpressibly fantastic, can ever be plausible again."

But in a radical departure from the recent past, Americans no longer had to rely on the words of Red Smith and columnists like him or disembodied voices on the radio to understand what happened at the Polo Grounds: They could watch it themselves, on their brand-new television sets. The rapid emergence of television coincided perfectly with the Thomson game. Four years earlier, the 1947 World Series had been the first to be televised; even then, it was broadcast only in the New York area (that series pitted the Yankees against the Dodgers). In fact, game 3 of the 1951 Dodgers-Giants playoff was the first major league baseball game in history to be broadcast coast-to-coast. As a result, millions of Americans witnessed the historic home run who otherwise would have been forced to just listen to it on the radio or read about it in the newspapers. Although radio broadcaster Russ Hodges's famous call of the home run—*"The Giants win the pennant! The Giants win the pennant!"*—is the one we hear today, the real significance of the moment is that millions of people across the country saw it with their own eyes.

The Thomson home run was, therefore, more than just a baseball moment—it was a media first. Because of the new popularity of television, news of Thomson's blast spread across America instantaneously, heralding a sea change in the way that people communicate. All the joy and pain were on display for anyone to see.

The television footage of the home run also guaranteed that the moment endured. Even today, more than half a century later, sports broadcasts and documentary films routinely show the grainy black-and-white footage of October 3, 1951. The footage is so familiar that even people who don't follow sports can recognize it, and baseball fanatics have had the details etched in their memories—Branca going into his windup, Thomson pulling the ball down the line and then skipping around the bases after seeing the ball clear the left-field wall, fans in the stands leaping to their feet in celebration, Giants manager Leo Durocher ripping his hat off his head and spinning in circles in sheer ecstasy.

It's not surprising that the home run inspired numerous literary and film references. The celebrated novelist John Steinbeck called it "the greatest game I or anyone else has ever seen" in a letter he wrote to Pascal Covici, his book editor for *East of Eden.* In 1959, Jack Kerouac wrote, "When Bobby Thomson hit that home run in 1951, I trembled with joy and couldn't get over it for days and wrote poems about how it is possible for the human spirit to win after all!" Philip Roth wrote about it in his satire of baseball and America, *The Great American Novel.*

But the most extensive use of the Thomson home run in literature is by Don DeLillo, who used the Thomson ball as the narrative thread for his sprawling 1997 modern classic *Underworld.* The novel opens with a sixty-page prologue (also published separately as a novella called *Pafko at the Wall*) centered entirely on October 3, 1951, at the Polo Grounds. The prologue even proposes a (fictional) solution to the mystery of what happened to the Shot Heard 'Round the World, showing a New York City kid named Cotter Martin grabbing the ball and running out of the stadium with it. One character in *Underworld* explains the aura that surrounds the missing artifact, saying, "Nobody has the ball. The ball never turned up. Whoever once had the ball, it never surfaced. This is part of the whole—what? The mythology of the game."

DeLillo's novel also features a character named Marvin Lundy, a memorabilia collector who devotes more than twenty years to obsessively hunting for the Thomson ball. Lundy relates how he took even "the skimpiest kind of lead" and pursued it "with a fury." I would soon come to understand the consuming nature of his quest.

The title character in Woody Allen's film *Deconstructing Harry,* clearly echoing Allen's own experience as a Giants' fan, says about the home run, "It was the first time I ever believed there was a God." In *The Godfather,* meanwhile, if you listen carefully during the scene when Sonny Corleone is gunned down at the tollbooths, you can hear Russ Hodges's voice from the Thomson game playing on the car radio as Sonny's last moments approach. The only problem with this scene is that it takes place in 1949—two years before the actual home run was hit. Director Francis Ford Coppola thought enough of the cultural significance of the moment to use his artistic license.

There was still another pop culture reference to the Thomson game, as I learned from my mother. One night she saw me feverishly taking notes by the TV and asked what I was doing. When I explained what I was researching, she excitedly told me, "Oh, I've got one for you. *M*A*S*H!*" Mom watched that show religiously, and she explained that an entire episode had been devoted to the 1951 season. "There was a great episode when Klinger convinces Winchester to bet on the Dodgers," she said. "Winchester listens and after Thomson hits the big home run, Winchester passes out beneath the loudspeaker broadcasting the game, clutching his Dodgers cap. You even hear the famous call."

I looked into this and sure enough, the *M*A*S*H* episode "A War for All Seasons," which originally aired in late 1980, unfolded just as she described.

The Thomson home run continued to capture the nation's imagination even fifty years after the fact. In 2001, the game became front-page news all across the country—again—when Joshua Prager of the *Wall Street Journal* wrote a story documenting how the '51 Giants had set up an elaborate system to steal opponents' signs. Prager claimed that Giants manager Leo Durocher put in place a telescope and buzzer system that let the Giants' batters know what pitches were coming, which fueled their phenomenal comeback that season—and even may have tipped off Bobby Thomson that Ralph Branca was throwing a fastball. The Prager story became big news from coast to coast, causing massive debate among sports fans: If the Giants really were cheating, did that mean the Thomson home run was tainted? Thomson now denies he ever got the sign.

It was a testament to the enduring legacy of the Shot Heard 'Round the World that the story could still command the country's attention half a century later. I now understood that the Thomson home run retained a hold over people. But I still needed to find the baseball itself or, better yet, a way to prove that my dad's ball was the one. Actually, I needed a place to *start* looking. I needed some clues.

•   •   •

WHAT BETTER PLACE to try to start unraveling the mystery, I reasoned, than in the museum that houses so many of baseball's treasures—the Baseball Hall of Fame in Cooperstown, New York. Curator Ted Spencer had been very helpful when my dad called the Hall of Fame about the Frick/Giles signature issue, so I decided to contact him. Ted graciously agreed to let me and my camera crew come up to Cooperstown to shoot some footage and have a look around the museum.

But then my demons threatened to undo the progress I had made. A few days before I was scheduled to travel, I experienced one of my worst panic attacks. I couldn't breathe for stretches of forty-five seconds at a time. My sister, Rebecca, drove an hour and fifteen minutes in Friday rush-hour traffic from her house in Woodbury, Long Island, to help me. Curled up in a ball, tears flowing down my face, I overheard her whisper to my father, "What do you want to do, Dad? I think we should take him back to the hospital."

"He's got an important trip for his film coming up," Dad whispered back.

"Look at him. How's he going to be able to do that? He's really bad."

"I'll go with him if I have to. That worked the last time."

As soon as I heard my dad say this, I thought, *How did I become this helpless?* But being confronted with my powerless state actually stirred some resolve in me.

"No! You can't drive me," I yelled. "It's five hours from here. Plus, what am I going to tell my crew? I'm going to be fine. I need to do this on my own, Dad. Please. Look, my breathing is already getting better. I'll be strong, just like you always tell me to be," I said, while gathering my composure.

I had spent the past few weeks readjusting to interacting with people on a professional level. Clearly I still hadn't fully emerged from the dark shadows of depression, anxiety, and self-loathing. The anticipation of being away from home had set off this massive wave of anxiety, which nearly swallowed me up. But there was too much at stake not to push on. I had made a pledge to my dad to find out the truth about his baseball. On the appointed day, I left for Cooperstown.

DRIVING THE WINDING roads of upstate New York en route to the Baseball Hall of Fame actually brought peace and clarity to my mind. It was a welcome visual change from the concrete canyons of the city. Looking out the window, I saw cows grazing and horses roaming on acres of farmland. My dad and I had talked about going to Cooperstown together many times but had never made the trip. Now I was going as more than just a tourist.

When I reached the Hall of Fame, Ted Spencer greeted me warmly on the lawn outside the museum. Ted was in his early sixties with longish, graying hair. He was wearing khakis with a long-sleeve, striped shirt and a green necktie. We set up a couple of lawn chairs right there outside the building and filmed our first conversation. Around us were brass statues of Johnny Podres and Roy Campenella in action from the Dodgers '55 championship season.

On the phone, I had told Ted simply that I was making a movie about the Thomson game but hadn't mentioned that I was looking for the ball. So I wanted to tread carefully during the early stages of the interview. First I asked him if he had any memory of the game. Responding in his thick Boston accent, he said, "Well, I'm lucky enough to be old enough to remember it. It was a special moment because it may have been the first thing we saw on TV in our house—1951 was the year we got a TV. I've always talked about

it as baseball's first TV event. That home run was played con-
tinually all that night. Remember, there's no satellite, there's no
twenty-four-hour-a-day news. News was fifteen minutes in those
days—6:00 to 6:15 local and 7:00 to 7:15 NBC. But it was all over
the place. It was big news. It was fabulous. I think from that point
on, baseball and TV really came together. In a lot of ways, it's a
much more important event than people understand."

Just say the phrase "the Shot Heard 'Round the World" to a
baseball fan, and he or she will immediately understand the reference to the famous home run. Not all fans could explain the origin
of the term, however. I asked Ted to fill in the background.

"It's a reference to the Revolutionary War," he said. More specifically, Ted explained that Ralph Waldo Emerson's famous poem
"Concord Hymn" described the musket round that began the Revolutionary War in 1775—setting the fledgling American colonies
against the mighty British empire—as "the shot heard round the
world." "Because the baseball game was broadcast on Armed Forces
Radio for soldiers overseas to hear," Ted noted, "it took on that
same sense of worldwide news."

Actually, the first headline the next day in the newspapers read
"The Shot Heard 'Round the *Baseball* World," but that was quickly
revised as the media realized how big an impact it had had around
the country and that it was not just a sports story, as I would later
learn.

Ted concluded, "As long as the stories of the game are told, Bobby
Thomson will be remembered. He will live forever because of that
home run."

The hundreds of thousands of visitors who make the pilgrim-
age to the Hall of Fame every year confirm the endless fascina-
tion with Thomson's blast. Bear in mind that the Hall of Fame is
the repository of the game's most sacred relics—from Babe Ruth's

sixtieth home-run ball to the jersey Hank Aaron wore when breaking Babe Ruth's home-run record in 1974, to a pair of spikes worn by Shoeless Joe Jackson, to Mickey Mantle's locker from old Yankee Stadium, to the silver trophy given to Lou Gehrig by his teammates, which he held up during his famous farewell speech in 1939.

And still, Spencer told me, "More people come to see [the Thomson exhibit] than anything else." Having seen countless visitors' reactions to the display, Ted understood the appeal: "If you walk by, you'll hear fathers and grandfathers explaining to kids about that moment and where they were. I think it's a great example of showing up for life every day, because you just never know when God is gonna say to you, *Okay, this is your day. See what you could do with it.* And that's what Thomson did. It's a wonderful story beyond just a guy hitting a home run in an important baseball game."

The Thomson display draws in so many visitors even though it does not feature the ball itself. I was extremely curious about what was preserved from the game. Ted told me: "We have the spikes he wore during the game, his hat, an old ticket stub, the rosin bag that Branca threw to the ground. We also have the bat, a thirty-four-ounce Adirondack, but it's on tour right now."

The absence of the ball offered me an opening to turn the conversation toward the real reason I had come to Cooperstown. "What do you know about what happened to the baseball?" I asked.

"That's been a mystery for all these years. We've had several people claim to have the ball, but none have been able to prove it."

"Do you think the ball will ever be found?"

"I don't know. I think if someone had it and knew they had it, it would have been resurrected and proven by now. It would be a monumental moment if we ever acquired it, but it's not something I think will happen. Too many years have gone by."

I had heard that sentiment expressed before, and it certainly did not bode well for my search. But when I asked whether only an auction house or curator could produce a ball that would be considered the one that Thomson actually hit, Ted offered me some hope.

"If a private individual came to us with a ball they claim to be authentic, we'd view it as having just as much validity as an auction house. It all depends on how much evidence they have. There's a lot more evidence out there than one might think. Information seems to be like 3-D matter. You almost can't destroy it; you just have to find it."

BUOYED BY SPENCER'S comments, I was eager to go see the actual Thomson exhibit. Ted introduced me to another Hall of Fame executive named Brad Horn. Brad was the senior communications director, a preppy, blond, handsome guy in his early thirties who spoke with a slight Southern drawl. He took me on a guided tour of the museum.

Brad walked me through the different sections of the the Hall, including the Babe Ruth room, the Hank Aaron display, and a room that had recently been set up called New York Baseball 1947–1957. I made certain to snap photos of the championship '55 Dodgers team to give to my dad.

Seeing all the incredible artifacts on display in the museum, many of them dating back to the early twentieth century, I found it even more difficult to believe that no one knew the fate of the Thomson ball. It didn't make sense that the most famous home-run ball ever could be unaccounted for when so many others were here.

As Brad led me toward the section I had traveled five hours to see, my attention was immediately drawn to a row of seats covered in chipped green paint on display in a corner. Brad must have seen the look on my face.

"I thought you'd be interested in those. They are original Polo Grounds seats. They were donated to the Hall after they tore the old stadium down."

Brad then led me up a carpeted staircase, and when we reached the top, he said, "It's just around this corner. Right past Mazeroski."

That would be Bill Mazeroski, who was responsible for a home run nearly as famous as Bobby Thomson's. Mazeroski, the Pittsburgh Pirates' light-hitting second baseman, sent the mighty New York Yankees to defeat in the 1960 World Series with his dramatic walk-off home run in the bottom of the ninth inning in game 7.

As Brad and I made a sharp turn around the corner, we moved into a darkened section and passed a display case with a photo of Mazeroski celebrating as he crossed home plate. Behind the glass, I saw Mazeroski's black helmet, the logo worn away, and his silver bat.

My anticipation grew. The idea of being in the presence of actual objects from the Thomson game made my heart pound and my stomach churn. Sure enough, just as Brad had promised, we came upon the display case for the famous 1951 Giants-Dodgers game.

Next to the large vertical glass display case was a black-and-white photograph of Thomson connecting with the ball. Taken from a bird's-eye view, the photo included a white dotted line that showed the home run's trajectory as it sailed into section 35. As I studied the picture, Brad launched into a presentation about the basic facts of the game, which he must have given a thousand times before but which he still told with interest. I particularly liked his description of the game's end: "Thomson gets up in the ninth inning with his team down two and hits a three-run home run that could have been a scene from a Hollywood movie. Fans swarm onto the field of the Polo Grounds trying to touch Thomson like he's the Pope, while his teammates carry him off the field in pandemonium. There is nothing else like it."

Turning my attention to the game-used items in the glass display—the Wilson spikes, faded black cap, beaten-up rosin bag, and yellowed ticket stub—I gently asked Brad the big question: "I see everything but the ball. Any clue where that is?"

"I get asked that question all the time—what happened to the Thomson ball? And my answer is always the same: It's truly a mystery. That ball just disappeared. It's funny, right across the way is the display of Bill Mazeroski's memorabilia. In many ways, his walk-off home run was just as spectacular, especially since it happened in the seventh game of the World Series. Yet everyone wants to come see the Shot Heard 'Round the World."

Brad was confirming what Ted Spencer had told me about the popularity of the Thomson game, but in the process he also hit on the same question that I had been pondering throughout my research—*Why* had the Thomson home run proved to be so legendary?

"There's such a sense of nostalgia surrounding that home run, it's palpable," Brad said. "The sheer drama of it. Russ Hodges's famous play-by-play call—'The Giants win the pennant! The Giants win the pennant!'—are probably the most famous words in baseball history. It feels like the legacy of that home run only gets bigger and will never fade."

As I spoke with Brad, I noticed out of the corner of my eye that a group of four women in their sixties had stopped to listen in. When we wrapped up the interview and shut off the cameras, one of the women, with short blond hair, long eyelashes, and a tan, approached me. "What kind of film are you making?" she asked.

I gave her what was becoming my standard line: "I'm making a documentary about Bobby Thomson's home run from 1951."

"Would you believe me if I told you I knew something about that?"

I figured someone from my production crew had sent her up as a joke, but I played along. "Oh really? And what's that?"

"I heard a company on Long Island was offering a $1 million reward for the missing baseball."

"You must have seen the story in the *Daily News*."

"Actually I heard about it from Bobby. I'm his girlfriend."

"What?! You're Bobby Thomson's *girlfriend*?"

She reached her hand out. "Hi, I'm Esther. Esther Daniels."

The way she looked me right in the eye as she spoke made me realize that this was no put-on. But what was she doing up in Cooperstown without Bobby?

"I'm up here on a golf outing," Esther told me, "and I wanted to show some of my friends the new display case."

I nodded politely at her golfing partners but quickly shifted my full attention to Esther. She seemed flattered, especially when my crew pointed their lights and cameras at her.

"Does Bobby ever talk about trying to get the ball back, or what might have happened to it?" I asked.

"Not to me. All I know is the ball was never found. People have claimed to have the ball. And there's all sorts of theories—but how would you prove such a thing? Bobby has dozens of balls from that era but not that one."

I had come to Cooperstown as the first step on my path, but I had no idea what the second step would be. Now my chance meeting with Esther was opening up an entirely new possibility: Maybe I could interview Bobby Thomson himself. I broached the subject with Esther, and she told me that he was always happy to talk about his place in baseball history. "It doesn't matter if you're a cub reporter or a big-shot Hollywood producer, Bobby treats everyone the same."

I couldn't believe my good luck in running into her. "It's pretty amazing that you're up here in Cooperstown the exact same day, the *only* day, that I'm here. And you brought your friends to the display case exactly when Brad brought me."

"It really is some coincidence, huh?" she said, shaking her head in disbelief.

I don't believe in coincidences. I believe that things happen for a reason. I know it sounds like something out of *Field of Dreams,* but I was suddenly overcome with the feeling that I was meant to meet Esther that day, that larger forces were somehow at work. I was starting to feel that I really could solve this mystery, that I would overcome all my recent setbacks in life as well as the obstacles that surely awaited me. I drove back to New York City more confident than before. Within a week, I had contacted Thomson and was ready to meet the legend.

Thomson swings at the second pitch from Branca, a high inside fastball, knocking it into the lower section (35) of the left-field stands, setting off pandemonium in the old Polo Grounds. *Courtesy of the Sporting News/ZUMA Press*

"The Whole World Will Know You"

Wednesday, October 3, 1951

It was the bottom of the ninth inning, and the score was 4-2, Dodgers. Bobby Thomson, the twenty-seven-year-old outfielder turned third baseman, stood in the on-deck circle and watched pitcher Don Newcombe. Thomson already had two hits on the day, but he was looking for any piece of information that might help him in his upcoming at bat against the tiring right-hander.

After Whitey Lockman doubled down the left-field line, Don Mueller slid into third base and began writhing in pain. Thomson and Mueller were very close friends, and Bobby ran, still holding the bat, from the on-deck circle to check on his teammate. Mueller had broken his ankle; he was carried off the field, and Giants utility player Clint Hartung was sent in to pinch-run. At that point the Giants' famously caustic manager, Leo Durocher, put his arm around Thomson—which had never happened before—and said, "Bobby, if you're ever gonna hit one, hit one now."

Thomson ambled over to the batter's box and dug in, thinking now as much about his buddy Mueller's health as the situation at hand. Thomson didn't even realize the Dodgers had made a pitching change until he looked up and saw Ralph Branca getting the sign from Rube Walker. The first pitch was a fastball down the middle. Thomson heard teammate Eddie Stanky yell from the dugout that he should have swung at it.

The count was 0-1.

Thomson stepped out of the batter's box, thinking to himself, Wait and watch. He repeated it like a mantra, even saying it out loud.

Branca kicked and dealt, and Thomson just jumped on the pitch, another fastball. When the ball left the bat he thought it would be a double off the wall, but it just kept going.

Thomson was ecstatic, of course—his team was headed to the World Series—but he didn't initially grasp the full scope of his accomplishment. After the clubhouse celebration, he rushed to see his big brother Jim, a fireman at Engine Company 154 on Staten Island. When Jim saw Bobby, he ran toward him, barely able to contain himself: "Bob, I can't believe what you did!"

Thomson, unfazed, replied, "It's just a home run."

Jim grabbed hold of his little brother. "Just a home run?! Bobby, you're going to be famous because of that one shot! Everyone with a TV was watching. Don't you realize, the whole world will know you. . . ."

IN THE DAYS leading up to my Thomson interview, I decided to learn as much about the man at the center of the mystery as possible. Robert Brown Thomson was born October 25, 1923, in Glasgow, Scotland. The youngest of six children, he came to the United States at the age of two, with his mother, Elizabeth, and his five older brothers and sisters. They settled in New York, where they joined his father, James, who had immigrated a year earlier.

James Thomson was a skilled cabinetmaker, and upon his arrival in New York, he immediately became a Brooklyn Dodgers fan. Like so many sons of New York, Bobby emulated his father and adopted the Dodgers as his favorite team. In fact, Bobby's first live baseball game was watching the Dodgers play in Ebbets Field at age seven or eight.

Thomson was raised on Staten Island. He got the nickname the Staten Island Scot while playing ball at Curtis High School.

An outstanding player, he was heavily recruited by the Dodgers. After his graduation in 1942, Bobby played on a team of "Dodger Rookies"—a collection of prospects the team was courting. It was essentially an extended tryout. Brooklyn used the team to look at the players before offering them contracts.

Thomson felt the Dodgers took it for granted that he would sign with them and was not pleased with what he called the arrogance of Dodgers executive Walter O'Malley. In the end, business was business, and the dyed-in-the-wool Dodger fan signed a contract with his team's archrival, the New York Giants, who made the better offer.

After just five games with the Giants' minor league team in Bristol, Virginia, Bobby moved on to Rocky Mount, North Carolina—both teams were class D, the same level my dad played in in Kentucky. As with so many other ballplayers of that era, World War II interrupted Thomson's career. In 1943, he was called up for active service, and he served as a bombardier in the Army Air Corps through 1945.

In 1946, his first year back in baseball, Bobby joined the Giants' AAA team—one step from the majors—at Jersey City, New Jersey. In Bobby's first game with Jersey City, the team played the Montreal Royals, who had recently signed a player named Jackie Robinson. It was *his* first game at AAA as well.

Bobby played extremely well for Jersey City, finishing the season with a team-record 26 home runs, and he landed with the big-league club for good in 1947. But he wasn't the most ballyhooed rookie in town that year—that honor would go to . . . Jackie Robinson. It was Robinson who won the Rookie of the Year award (the first ever given), though the young Giants outfielder actually put up more impressive numbers. Thomson batted .283 and had 29 home runs and 85 RBIs. Robinson's power numbers were much lower (12 home runs, 48 RBIs), but he swiped 29 bases, hit .297, collected 175 hits, and drew a lot more walks. (Thomson, in fact, finished third in the Rookie of the Year balloting, behind Jackie and Bobby's teammate, pitcher Larry Jansen.)

Thomson and Robinson weren't done crossing paths at crucial moments in their careers (and in baseball history): Jackie was manning second base when Bobby drove Branca's pitch over the left-field wall to end the 1951 season.

Despite emerging as one of the Giants' top players, Thomson didn't complain when manager Leo Durocher approached him in the middle of the 1951 pennant chase and told him the team was moving him from the outfield to third base because they wanted to play a rookie with blazing speed in center field. That rookie was Willie Mays.

I had already gotten a sense of Thomson's modesty from the way his girlfriend, Esther, talked about him and from reading a *New York Times* article by Ira Berkow, who reported that when asked how an old fan had found his contact information, Thomson replied, "I'm in the phone book. I'm nobody special." With that attitude, perhaps it's no surprise that Thomson didn't do much to fight for a big raise after the '51 season, when he set a career high with 32 home runs—including, of course, the Shot Heard 'Round the World. But when the bashful Thomson informed Durocher during the off-season that he had been offered only a slight pay raise by stingy Giants owner Horace Stoneham, the feisty manager stepped in. Two days later Thomson got the raise he deserved.

After his shining moment in '51, Bobby played two more seasons with the Giants, continuing to hit the long ball and knock in runs. In 1952, he slammed 24 home runs and had 108 RBIs; in 1953, he clocked 26 dingers with 106 RBIs. But the Giants needed pitching badly, and in the winter of 1953–54, Stoneham shipped off his household name to the Milwaukee Braves in a multiplayer deal; the Giants got back a package that included future 20-game winner Johnny Antonelli. The following year, the Giants won their only World Series of that era. Thomson has said that he had no regrets about the trade after the Giants won the Series, but years later, he felt cheated (he told me) that he had never tasted a championship. One interesting footnote about his time in Milwaukee: During his first spring training with the Braves, he suffered a broken ankle. His injury allowed rookie Hank Aaron, the future home-run king, to earn a place in the Milwaukee lineup instead of a bus ticket back to the minors.

The Braves traded Thomson back to the Giants during the 1957 season, and he was on the field for the club's final game at the Polo Grounds. The Giants moved to San Francisco for the 1958 season, but Thomson was gone, traded to the Cubs. He spent two seasons in Chicago before closing out his career in the American League with the Red Sox and Orioles. He played only three games for Baltimore before he retired, saying, "I just lost my love for playing. It was feeling like a job and not a passion, so it was time to hang 'em up."

Bobby Thomson finished his career a .270 hitter, with 264 home runs and 1,026 RBIs in 1,779 games. Impressive, no doubt. But had he not come through against Branca on that October day in 1951, only the most obsessed baseball fans would know his name today. Bobby's brother Jim was right: It was much more than just a home run.

As I drove to Bobby Thomson's home in Watchung, New Jersey, I thought about the questions I would ask: Obviously I wanted to know about the ball, but I was also interested in hearing his memories of all the Dodger players my parents grew up worshipping.

Thomson's ranch-style house reflected the same modesty that the man showed. It was painted white and had a small, well-manicured lawn with a signpost planted in the grass—the swinging shingle read: R. B. THOMSON. As I pulled my car onto his quiet, tree-lined suburban block, I could see him, hands in his pockets, slowly pacing up and down his driveway. He was waiting for me, like a grandpa anticipating the arrival of his grandchildren.

Dressed in a neatly tucked purple golf shirt, pleated pants, and white sneakers, he greeted me with a firm handshake. He was taller than I expected. I'm six two, but somehow it felt as though he towered over me even though we're supposedly the same height. A month shy of his eighty-third birthday, he was hale and hearty and had a gentle way about him. He squinted through his square, thin-framed eyeglasses down at my business card, then graciously directed the crew toward the back entrance. He and I slowly followed them in, chatting all the while.

I don't know exactly what I was hoping Thomson would tell me, but I figured that at least he could confirm that the team had signed the home-run ball. Ideally, he might have some memory of the person who caught it: Maybe he met the lucky fan after the game or even saw the person as he rounded the bases. But I didn't want to broach the subject until the cameras were rolling, so we nestled ourselves at a table in the living room, continuing to make small talk while the crew set up in his den. He told me he had lost his wife about a dozen years earlier, and I shared my experience of meeting Esther in Cooperstown.

"Oh, she's a wonderful gal. She gets along so well with my family. She and my daughter take turns coming to the house to tidy up. I'm not so good at the housework," he said, smirking.

Unlike many players, Thomson never went into broadcasting or pursued a life in baseball after his playing days. Instead, he worked for a paper company as a salesman. He did mention to me that over the years, he and Ralph Branca appeared together signing autographs at memorabilia shows like the one my dad had met him at. When he mentioned memorabilia, I nearly brought up the ball, but I wanted to be certain he was comfortable talking with me. So we talked about—what else?—baseball.

"How did you get interested in baseball?" I asked him.

"I have my older brother Jimmy to thank for that," pointing to a fireman plaque with Jim's name etched in it. "He bought me my first glove. I actually liked playing soccer more, but Jimmy taught me the fundamentals of hitting and throwing in the backyard of our Staten Island home when I was a kid. I took to it right away."

Thomson had played against so many all-time greats, including my parents' favorites on the Brooklyn Dodgers. One of those players was, of course, Jackie Robinson, whose career was entwined with his at so many key moments. I couldn't resist asking whether he ever felt unlucky to have been a rookie at the same time as Jackie. He smiled as I said, "Most other years you'd have been Rookie of the Year with a .283 average, 29 homers, and 85 RBIs." Bobby, who was never fleet of foot, jokingly reminded me, "I had one stolen base my rookie year, though."

I also asked about my dad's all-time favorite, the Jewish lefty from Brooklyn's Lafayette High, Sandy Koufax. Thomson grinned at me while pointing to a spot on his forearm.

"See this spot? He once hit me here with a curveball that was so fast it left a mark for three days. It looked like I had the stitches of a baseball tattooed on my arm."

"How about Snider, what do you remember about him?"

"The Duke of Flatbush—a real leader and fierce competitor. I know Duke was really hard on himself, always wanted to be the best. When he was a rookie, he knocked in close to a hundred RBIs but had a terrible World Series against the Yankees, and *that's all he thought about.* Someone once told me that he actually considered quitting after that."

Even though Thomson looked comfortable and relaxed, I was well aware of the lack of confidence and self-assuredness that had consumed him in his playing days. "I suppose I have been too timid," he told *Sport* magazine in 1955. "There never was much tiger or whatever you want to call it in me."

What was it like, then, for such an unassuming man to become one of the most famous players on the planet? How did his life change after the home run?

"Geez," he told me, "there wasn't a restaurant or train or bus I could go on without someone asking me for my autograph or to shake my hand. They even wanted my mom's signature. Even on the road, reporters would be waiting in the hotel for interviews, and photographers were snapping shots like I was a movie star or something. It was crazy. 'Take some of [Whitey] Lockman, or Willie [Mays], or [Sal] Maglie—they're the real stars,' I would tell them. I'm not much for all the hoopla, but it came with the territory."

Crossing his long legs, Thomson continued, "Heck, even when I was traded to Milwaukee, it followed me. I guess I was a national star, but I just didn't really know what that meant. . . . I remember in Milwaukee the local grocers and gas station attendants never let me pay. My daughter was quite young at the time and didn't understand it all. But I guess worse things could happen, right?"

Bobby revealed his humility as he talked about life in the spotlight. After the 1951 World Series against the Yankees, still in the glow of the Shot Heard 'Round the World, he appeared on *The*

Ed Sullivan Show. "I was not so comfortable," Thomson told me. "I knew anyone with a TV set would be watching." Bobby went on the show along with several other players, from both the Giants and the Yankees. "I remember the announcer saying, 'Now introducing America's biggest star,' and I looked around to see who they were talking about. It was me!"

Thomson's eyes opened wide, as if the moment had just occurred.

He was just as self-effacing when I asked him about the TV commercials and other endorsement deals that came his way. "I was a terrible actor," he said, "but so many sponsors wanted me on their products, which I thought was kind of silly." Pressed for details, he rattled off a list of products he had endorsed: Rheingold Beer, Coca-Cola, Armstrong Tires, Bromo-Seltzer, "one of the big chewing-tobacco companies." He also explained that he was called to do speaking engagements, "which is ironic because I'm really shy by nature."

"What would you say was your favorite product endorsement?" I asked.

Letting out a sheepish smile, he replied, "Don't laugh, but they actually made a comic book about me. They sketched this big muscular guy with a huge square jaw that was supposed to look like me, and it was called something like *The Story of a Baseball GIANT.*"

"Do you still have it?"

"I'm not much into keeping those things. My daughter might have it somewhere. I do have a bunch of 33-cent 'Shot Heard 'Round the World' postage stamps, though. That was probably one of my biggest honors."

As Bobby described all that had happened to him, and the way people still wanted to talk about October 3, 1951, all these years later, I realized that it was a dramatic understatement when he told me, "The home run changed my life forever."

OUR CONVERSATION HAD been lively and fascinating, but I still hadn't asked Thomson about the famous missing baseball. I needed to get him in front of the camera for that. Finally my assistant signaled to me that we were ready to begin shooting. Bobby and I walked into the den.

"I hope you didn't use up your best material back there," I kidded him.

"I hope so, too," he said with sincerity. "Sorry if I was rambling."

I didn't ask about the sign-stealing allegations because I didn't want to put him on the defensive. After starting off with some questions about the 1951 regular season, I asked him to take me back to the famous at bat and walk me through what he heard and saw. He must have been asked that question a million times, but his face lit up as if the moment had just happened and this was the first time he'd ever described it. In retrospect, he told me, Don Mueller's injury was a blessing in disguise—Thomson was so concerned about his friend's health that he forgot the pressure.

He knew he had put a good swing on Branca's pitch, but he didn't realize it would be a home run. "When it left the bat, I first thought it would be a double off the wall, but it just kept going. Even though the pitch was inside, I was able to get around on it and get some good wood on it."

I asked him if he looked up into the outfield to follow the flight of the ball.

"No. It was a sinking line drive. It flew over Pafko's head and into the seats in a blink."

"How about during your home-run trot, did you look up then?"

"As I was rounding the bases, my feet were not touching the ground. I was floating in midair. I didn't see anything."

The players carried him off the field. "I felt like I was riding a bucking bronco."

Now it was time for the big question: "Did you ever find out what happened to the ball?"

He answered in a soft voice, "I have a story about that."

WHEN I HEARD those words, I got a lump in my throat. Maybe he had the details I had been looking for.

The very next day, Thomson explained, the World Series was set to begin against the Yankees. "I drove my Mercury to Yankee Stadium," he told me, and "when I got out of the car a guy quickly approached me in the parking lot and said, 'Bobby, I have that ball you hit yesterday, and I'll give it to you for two tickets to today's game.' I told him, 'Wait right here,' and led him toward the tunnel in front of the player's entrance. I rushed inside and found our clubhouse manager, Eddie Logan, and told him why I needed two extra tickets. He just laughed at me. 'What are you laughing at? The guy's waiting outside.' 'Look over there,' Logan said. A few of the players milling around the locker room chuckled under their breath. 'Over where?' Eddie brought me over to my locker. When I opened it, about eight baseballs came spilling out. Each one was dropped off by fans looking for tickets who claimed *they* caught my home run."

I was supposed to be amused by his story but couldn't be—I was looking for answers, not anecdotes. I nervously asked, "Whatever happened to those eight baseballs?"

"I don't have any idea. Eddie would be the only guy who would know that."

I asked Bobby if anyone else had ever contacted him claiming to have knowledge about the missing baseball. He told me that in the winter of '51, more than one person mailed him ticket stubs from section 35 and wanted to meet with him to give him back his famous ball for a reward. But he figured they were just scam artists and ignored them. After the locker-room incident, he gave up hope of recovering it.

"Bobby, do you remember autographing any baseballs after the game or even during the World Series from a fan claiming they caught your home run? Maybe you didn't believe them but signed it anyway?"

Thomson shook his head. He clearly didn't remember signing the baseball. I decided to take one last stab at jogging his memory and asked him point blank, "So you're sure that you and the other guys on the team didn't sign the ball at some point?"

"Definitely not after the game—I'd remember that. Who knows how many balls I signed over the years?"

We wrapped up our conversation, and I realized that I'd just heard it straight from the man himself: The team did not sign his home-run ball during any period after the game. This was bad news for my dad. His whole case that he had the ball was based on the idea that the team had signed the ball on or near the day of the game.

But my dad didn't put much stock in my report. He still believed. "It was fifty years ago!" he said when I told him of Thomson's recollection. "Maybe he doesn't remember, or maybe he doesn't want to admit it. He didn't sign the ball just like Warren Giles's stamp is supposed to be on the ball. Maybe they were all drunk! Ballplayers were big drinkers in those days."

After the Lelands debacle, Dad was not ready to trust anyone's claims about the ball. I could feel his pain and humiliation the same way I'm sure he felt mine during my lowest times. I wasn't convinced that his ball was *the* ball, but that didn't matter anymore; my journey was just beginning. One way or another, I would find out what happened to that baseball. And now I had another lead. I had to find Eddie Logan.

Searching for Eddie Logan

Wednesday, October 3, 1951

Eddie Logan Jr. wasn't like every other ten-year-old Giants fan. He got special privileges because his father, Eddie Sr., was the clubhouse manager. His dad was in charge of supplying the players with various sundries before and after games—Hershey bars, Coca-Cola, Wrigley's chewing gum, and pouches of chewing tobacco. He was also responsible for cleaning the uniforms, and making sure that all the appropriate gear made it with the team when they traveled by plane, train, or bus.

Eddie Jr. was practically raised in the Giants' clubhouse. Almost every weekend and most days during the summer when the Giants were in town, he'd go where he wanted in the clubhouse, on the field, and throughout the stadium. Everyone knew "Logan's kid." He would show up for games at the Polo Grounds and go in through the center-field entrance on the Eighth Avenue side. He'd take the short staircase up toward the main clubhouse floor. On the right was Leo Durocher's office, and from there he'd make a left and go up a few more stairs to the Giants' locker room. Unlike many major league ballparks, the Polo Grounds had its locker rooms situated aboveground within the bowels of the outfield bleachers. Inside, it smelled like rubbing alcohol and Ben-Gay. There were some spittoons scattered about, and you could see and smell tobacco juice everywhere.

Eddie Sr. was a second-generation clubbie. His father, Fred, was the first clubhouse manager at Yankee Stadium when it opened in 1923. He was thrilled to have Eddie Jr. around the Polo Grounds, but he didn't want his son to follow in his footsteps as he had his father's. And so, on the day of the deciding playoff game, Eddie

Giants clubhouse manager Eddie Logan Sr. straightens up shortstop Alvin Dark's locker. *From the author's collection*

Sr. ignored Eddie Jr.'s pleas to attend, saying, "It's a school day and you have to go. I want you to go to college and not have to clean jocks the rest of your life like me."

Reluctantly, ten-year-old Eddie rode his bike to school up at PS 11 in the Bronx, in the heart of Yankee country. It was only two blocks from his apartment, and he prayed that his fifth-grade teacher, Mrs. Ceder, would let the kids out early to go home to watch or listen to the game. But Principal Olsen declared: "No kids are to leave early to try to see the game. They're too young to miss school."

Eddie begged Mrs. Ceder to make an exception for him, but to no avail. Trying to make the best of a bad situation, he figured, since he lived so close and had his bike with him, that he could still be home in time to catch the last few innings on the radio. And that's exactly what happened. School let out at three o'clock, and he was listening to the game in the bottom of the seventh inning with his six-year-old brother, Roger, who had no idea what was going on.

Immediately after Thomson's blast, Eddie jumped on his bike and sped across to the Polo Grounds. Usually he was able to get right into the clubhouse to see his dad, but not on this day. There was pandemonium all around the park, and he couldn't make it through the delirious crowd of Giants fans. He headed back home, disappointed he didn't get in, but still thrilled by the fact that his dad's team was going to the World Series for the first time in his life.

He tried to stay awake long enough to talk to his dad when he got home, but Eddie Sr. didn't wind up coming home that night because he was so busy packing up the equipment for the trip to Yankee Stadium for the World Series, which started the very next day.

I HAD A call in to the Giants' alumni representative to get contact information for Eddie Logan Sr. While I was waiting to hear back, I accompanied one of my executive producers, Sal Del Giudice, on a location scout to an indoor batting range being built in Port Washington, Long Island. I was feeling better and better about reconnecting with my professional life, and Sal and I were developing a reality TV series about high school baseball players trying to get noticed by professional scouts.

While walking through the state-of-the-art indoor sports facility, still under construction, we were approached by a man named Nuzzolese. He never told us his first name. Everyone called him Nuzzo, he said. Nuzzo was a tough-looking Italian guy in his late sixties, dressed in a tight-fitting T-shirt and jeans. He could have played Paulie Walnuts's brother on *The Sopranos*. After some small talk, Nuzzo asked us what we were doing there.

"We might want to shoot some sample footage here for a TV show once the place is finished," I told him.

"You'll have to talk to Al. He's the owner. What other shows do you guys make?"

"Have you ever heard of the Shot Heard 'Round the World?"

Eddie Logan Sr. alone in the locker room, located under the center-field bleachers of the Polo Grounds. *From the author's collection*

"*Minchia!* Fuhgedaboudit! . . . Are you kiddin' me? . . . Fuckin' Bobby Thomson. He should get horned by the devil."

After Sal and I stopped laughing, I explained that we were making a film that goes in search of the missing baseball—worth over a million dollars.

"A million bucks?! That's a lotta *'scaroles*. You think you're gonna find it?"

"Right now we're just trying to find the old Giants clubhouse manager, Eddie Logan."

Before I could finish my sentence, Nuzzo was dialing his cell phone.

"Talk to Mickey," he said, handing me his phone. "He'll give you whatever you need."

The phone was already ringing before I could ask, "Who is Mickey?"

"Mickey Rendine. He was the clubbie for the Yankees in the fifties. He knows everything about everybody from baseball."

A raspy, tired voice answered the other end of the phone. Rendine was well into his eighties.

"Nuzzo, what did I tell you about calling me during the afternoon? I like to take a nap. I was just about to fall asleep, you prick."

"Hi, Mickey. This actually isn't Nuzzo . . ."

Nuzzo was right about Mickey. He knew all about the Logans and told me that Eddie Logan Sr. had passed away in the midnineties. I felt deflated. How would I track down one of those eight baseballs with Logan gone?

A FEW DAYS later, I got a call from the San Francisco Giants that revitalized me and the Logan lead. Both of Logan's sons, Eddie Jr. and Roger, had worked for the team in the fifties and were alive and well. Eddie Jr. was actually the Giants' batboy in 1957, the final year before the team moved to San Francisco. I was also informed that Roger currently had a memorabilia room in the Monroe Residence Club Hotel in San Francisco, where he worked as the manager. This was great news: If he collected memorabilia, I figured he was certain to be willing to help me. If anyone knew what happened to those eight baseballs that Logan put in Thomson's locker, it would be him or his brother. My goal was to find the balls from that day. From there, perhaps there might be some scientific way to determine which one was the one used in the game.

I made calls to both brothers, and Roger called me back first. He was too young to have any memories from the day, but I still had plenty of questions to ask him. His voice was deep and he spoke fast, as if things were just popping into his head, nearly rambling but still coherent. As was my pattern, I wanted to get him talking about the era before I asked him specifically what he knew about the ball.

I was particularly curious about his relationship with Leo Durocher. Knowing Leo's reputation, I was guessing that maybe he wasn't thrilled about always having the clubbie's kids around. To my surprise, Roger spoke fondly of the Lip. Despite Leo's intimidating approach to players, umpires, and the world in general, Roger said he was a very gentle and devoted man off the field. Leo didn't drink or smoke but was not shy about cursing. (I came across a fantastic example of Durocher's artful approach to profanity in my research. He was the Dodgers' manager during Jackie Robinson's rookie year, and when he was questioned about penciling in the name of a black man in the lineup, he said, "I don't care if the guy is yellow or black, or if he has stripes like a fucking zebra. I'm the manager of this team, and I say he plays.")

According to Roger, Durocher was all business once the call-to-order bell in the Giants' dugout sounded, alerting the players that the game was about to start. Leo was always the first one in the clubhouse every morning—except for Eddie Sr. One early Saturday morning, Eddie Sr. designed a uniform for little Roger to wear featuring Giants legend Mel Ott's number 4. Not thinking anyone would see, the father and son proudly pranced around the clubhouse in the early hours of the morning when Leo, who arrived six hours before game time that day, interrupted them. The Logans assumed that the fiery manager would chew them out for making noise and carrying on. But before Eddie Sr. could speak, Durocher gave him a big smile. "Ed, your son's ready to go. I like that." Leo walked off to his office, while the Logans rejoiced.

I asked Roger if he always lived in fear of upsetting Durocher.

"Dad told Eddie Jr. and me not to bother the players. We were taught to respect everyone, especially Leo, and not get in their way."

Then he told me his best Durocher story: For as long as Roger could remember, Leo was always trashing the Dodgers. The bad feelings between the two teams extended beyond the fans back then—they were real. This was particularly so for Durocher, who had managed the Dodgers for the better part of a decade and had had a cantankerous relationship with upper management even when he worked for them. Based on Leo's constant refrains about how awful the Dodgers were, young Roger envisioned them to be monsters.

One day in 1957, when the Dodgers were playing at the Polo Grounds, Eddie Sr. needed to deliver visitors' passes to the opposing team's locker room. He brought twelve-year-old Roger with him. Roger was terrified to go inside. He imagined a room full of the nasty men that Leo always talked about. He nervously hung on to his dad's pocket and entered the Dodgers' locker room. Eddie Sr. drifted away to do his job, and Roger was left standing all alone. A short, round-faced man with squinty little eyes approached Roger, and the boy's mouth went dry—he was expecting a tongue lashing for loitering or spying. But Pee Wee Reese knew he was the clubbie's son and was just coming by to say hello. He offered Roger a stick of Wrigley's chewing gum and an unreserved smile. To this day, Roger says that Pee Wee was the nicest guy he ever met in baseball. Shortly after, Eddie Sr. rounded up Roger, and father and son exited the enemy's turf.

"Daddy, Daddy," he said, "the Dodgers have this really nice man on their team. It's not true what Leo says. They're human beings—just like us."

I asked him about other memories from that time. He told me all about the area inside the stadium behind center field, where various celebrities used to gather and watch through a row of field-level windows. He remembered meeting Danny Kaye, Jerry Lewis,

Frank Sinatra, and Dean Martin. It sounded like quite a scene, with the celebs mixing with the police, clergy, and reporters. They would all watch from out there just because it was a fun place to be, with lots of booze and cigar smoke, like an old speakeasy. When Roger was nine years old, Jerry Lewis gave him a pen with a legend on it: "Stolen from Jerry Lewis."

He might not have any memory from the '51 game, but surely he'd heard his dad and brother and the various Giants players talk about it a thousand times. Maybe he remembered something important. When I asked, though, all he came up with was a funny story: "My Dad told me that after Thomson hit the home run, reporters flocked around Sinatra, who was sitting near the dugout that day. His quote was, 'I didn't know you could have so much fun during the day.'"

I decided to get more specific: "Did your dad ever talk about what happened to the Thomson ball?"

"My dad made a lot of money off that."

This was a twist I wasn't expecting. I asked him to explain.

"I remember a day in 1954. I went to the ballpark with Dad and saw this fan waiting for him near the players' entrance. The stranger approached him, and they had a hushed conversation. Then he walked off into the clubhouse, reappearing with a used bat. He sold the bat to the guy, telling him it was the one Thomson used in the '51 game. He pulled the same stunt over and over again."

Afterward, Eddie Sr. would chortle—and pocket the cash. For years after the Thomson game, Eddie Sr. was selling Thomson memorabilia to various naive fans, both in New York and on the road. Apparently, he wasn't the most ethical guy in the world, to say the least.

I loved talking to Roger and getting such an intimate account of what it was like to be so chummy with pro players from the fifties.

Unfortunately, I hadn't gotten any closer to my real goal. I was hoping I'd get further by talking to Eddie Jr.

WHEN I GOT Eddie Jr. on the phone, I quickly learned that his privileges were good both on and off the field. When Eddie was twelve years old, he was chosen to babysit for Durocher's five-year-old adopted son, Chris, while Leo was running the ball club. Eddie would play ball with Chris on the field and hang out with him in the clubhouse. As a reward for doing such a good job with Chris, Durocher bought Eddie Jr. a brand-new Schwinn bicycle. The bike was delivered to Durocher's office, and he called Eddie in to give it to him. "Durocher was like General Grant running that clubhouse," Eddie told me. "When he gave me the bike, I actually saw a side of him I didn't know existed."

Usually, Eddie's father discouraged him from hanging out too much around the players—they had important work to do, and he didn't want his son to monopolize their time. But there were players who genuinely enjoyed hanging out with kids in the clubhouse or in the neighborhood. One such player was the twenty-year-old rookie Willie Mays (who was on deck when Thomson hit the home run). Mays lived on St. Nicholas Avenue and 155th Street, not far from the Polo Grounds. Eddie would ride his bike over to visit him. Apparently, being a budding major league star wasn't enough for Mays—he also had a passion for stickball. Eddie would show up, and there would already be several neighborhood kids playing. In the late summer of 1951, Willie would often play a day game at the Polo Grounds and then stickball with Eddie and other local kids at night.

Later in the fifties, Eddie frequently warmed up Mays before games by playing long toss in the outfield. Willie was a sweetheart of a man, Eddie told me, and liked to joke with the kid. He would purposely throw the ball as hard as he could to see if he could knock Eddie's mitt off or if Eddie would give up. Whenever Eddie cringed in pain from a stinging shot to the palm, Willie would say, "Don't give up on your drum-playing career, Logan."

Mays was very superstitious. In 1957, the year Eddie was the batboy, Willie would insist that Eddie sit in the on-deck circle with him. Early in the season, Eddie rubbed the bat for good luck, and Mays knocked one over the fence. The rest of the season, Eddie would have to rub the bat in the same way before each time Mays stepped to home plate. "Rub it down, Eddie. You know the routine."

When it was time for Eddie to go to college, his dad was not making a lot of money and couldn't afford the tuition to send Eddie to Arizona State. Mays gave the money to Eddie Sr. and so he was able to send his boy off to the school he had his heart set on. Mays knew he'd never see the return of his loan and was fine with that.

I was fascinated to hear Eddie's and Roger's stories about growing up with the Giants. As the son of die-hard Dodgers fans, I had been steeped in Brooklyn's tradition, in the bond that Brooklynites felt with the players, in the impact that pivotal games had on their lives. But in listening to Eddie and Roger speak, I understood just how meaningful those Giants teams were to their fans. Eddie spoke of Willie Mays the same way my father recalled his brushes with Duke Snider. I had known the pain that Thomson had caused Dodgers fans, but now I could really appreciate the sheer exhilaration that he had brought to Giants fans like young Eddie.

Of course, there still remained the crucial matter of the ball itself. This is where I hoped Eddie Jr. would come in. Finally I dropped my most important question: What happened to those eight baseballs that his dad put in Thomson's locker the day after the game?

Eddie's response was crushing: "They were probably used for batting practice that day. They weren't put in a special bag because nobody believed the real ball was there anyway. And back then, people didn't know that the ball would have any real value. Dad was a big jokester, so he probably thought the fans were playing a joke as well. I wish he would have saved them."

EDDIE WAS MATTER-OF-FACT in saying that the eight baseballs were long gone, and his comment made perfect sense. Looking back, in fact, I can't imagine I expected any other response from him. But I was so determined to see this project through that I just refused to believe that Eddie Sr. could have let the balls go so easily. I spoke to the Logan brothers several more times after I got this deflating news, still thinking that maybe one of them could provide a clue—even indirectly—to bring me closer to solving the mystery. Maybe there was some small detail that their father may have mentioned, a detail they might have initially forgotten.

Roger's memorabilia room in the hotel, loaded with tangible links to baseball's past, became an obsession of mine. Part of me was convinced that Logan might have the Thomson baseball and just not know it, improbable as that sounds. I asked Roger for a detailed description of the room and its collection. Roger's biggest source of pride was his dad's 1954 World Series ring. Other items on display included one of Alvin Dark's bats, snapshots of Leo Durocher and his wife, Laraine Day (little Chris's mom), and a small satchel that belonged to longtime pitching coach and scout Frank Shellenback. In those days, before each game, players and coaches would put their personal belongings in a little canvas pouch with their names inked on it, and the clubhouse manager would lock all the pouches in a trunk. Roger held on to Shellenback's satchel all these years because it was a unique little item—one that only the kid of a clubhouse manager could appreciate. He did tell me he had several signed baseballs from various years. Unfortunately, none of them were to be candidates for the Thomson ball.

As much as I pressed both Logans for more information, there was none to be had. That's when I started to get worried. My first lead had not panned out. Despite all I had learned, I was really no closer to solving the riddle than the day I started. I was at my first dead end. It would not be my last.

CSI: Polo Grounds

Ideas can come from anywhere. And sometimes the least likely sources are the ones that bear the most fruit. Unsatisfied with my results from talking to the Logan brothers, I was contemplating flying to San Francisco to meet with Roger and go over every inch of his memorabilia room. Could there be even a small clue hidden within his collection? Could one of the unidentified baseballs he mentioned be the original? My mom dropped a heavy dose of reality on me one night when I was ranting about how I was going to go out to San Francisco and come back with the ball. I was sitting on the top step of the basement landing, and Mom was standing in the doorway, urging me to come into the kitchen to eat.

In a gentle voice, Mom told me, "Brian, Roger Logan would know if he had that ball. And even if you find some random ball, how are you going to know it is the right one? Roger told you that the balls he has from that era had no markings on them. They might not even be professional baseballs."

It was a valid point. The next night, we resumed the conversation after dinner while watching the TV show *NCIS* in the living room.

A unique look inside the Polo Grounds from the right-field seats, circa 1950. *Andreas Feininger, courtesy of the Museum of the City of New York*

Mom watched it every Tuesday night and eventually got me and my dad hooked. The lead character, Special Agent Gibbs, is played by Mark Harmon, who started at quarterback for the UCLA Bruins in the early 1970s.

Glancing at the TV, I half jokingly said, "Hey, Ma, what do you think Gibbs would do if he were in my situation?"

At first she just laughed. Then she thought for a second and with

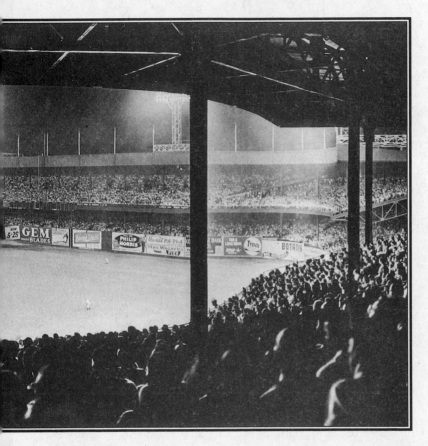

a curled eyebrow she said, "You know, in all seriousness, I bet there is a way you could take a forensics approach to finding this ball." I sat back on the couch, letting the idea sink in. I glanced at my dad. He remained silent. "You know, you might be right," I said to Mom in a stunned whisper. "Maybe there's a scientific way to examine Thomson's bat—see if there is some way to match it up with Dad's baseball—or any other ball."

I thought of one hitch in the plan right away. Thomson's bat was actually touring the country as part of a traveling Hall of Fame exhibit, and I seriously doubted that they would allow me to perform any tests on it anyway. I mentioned this to my mom, and once again, her response made so much sense I couldn't believe I hadn't already thought of it myself. "Why don't you use your forensic approach to analyze the evidence that you *do* have before flying all over the country looking for the bat?

It was a brilliant idea. I had a few pieces of evidence already in hand. There was a photo from the *Daily News,* printed back in 1951, titled *Pafko at the Wall,* which showed section 35 right after the home run. What if I could use today's technology to analyze this picture to find a clue as to who caught the ball? At the very least, I thought I might be able to narrow it down to a few suspects. Then maybe I could hire a private investigator to track down the relevant people.

I wasn't satisfied with just one photo, though. So I spent the next few weeks searching for others, while at the same time looking for more clues in the archival game footage sent to me by a contact I'd made at Major League Baseball. I spent many late nights alone in the edit room analyzing every detail of the famous home run, frame by frame. Unfortunately, in the 1950s, TV networks didn't have eight different cameras with super-slow-motion showing every conceivable angle, as in today's broadcasts. There wasn't a camera shot that stayed on section 35 long enough to reveal any tangible evidence, so I focused all my energy on searching for other photographs.

I looked for old sports pictures practically every place I could think of—on the Internet, at vintage poster shops in the East Village, used-book stores down near Union Square—you name the place. I stumbled on all kinds of weird stuff, including a laminated picture of Starsky and Hutch hopping over their red Gran Torino with the white racing stripe. There were also several framed velvet unicorns, a picture of Rodney Dangerfield with his real name,

Jacob Cohen, in parentheses, and a book my mother used to read to me when I was a kid, called *Barney Beagle Plays Baseball.*

One Saturday afternoon, my dad and I drove to the Tri-County Flea Market in Levittown, Long Island, where there was a large sports memorabilia section, including an impressive array of baseball cards, autographed publicity pictures, game-used apparel, and a large assortment of photos, old and new.

Dad pointed me toward a table with old wooden crates loaded with sports photos—some dating back to the early forties. Something about those wooden crates, filled with photographic masterpieces, seemed magical, each shot so perfectly capturing an exact moment in time and making it come alive for me. There was a classic shot of Tony Zale knocking out Rocky Graziano in 1946 in the first of their many great fights. There was a great picture of Roger Staubach on the sidelines in his rookie year (1969), listening to instructions from legendary coach Tom Landry, who was dressed in his usual checkered sport jacket and trademark fedora. While flipping through pictures as if they were LPs or CDs in a music store, I came across a real hidden gem. It was a black-and-white horizontal glossy print. At first I thought it was *Pafko at the Wall.* In fact, it was almost identical. But as I examined it, I realized that the angle wasn't the same. This shot was wider and was taken from the third-base side. I could tell from the position of Pafko's body that this image was snapped just a second or two after the *Daily News* shot. Pafko's head was looking toward the infield in this one, probably at Thomson rounding the bases, not up at the ball sailing over his head. There was no photo credit anywhere on the mint-condition 8 × 11, but that made no difference to me, as I was now in possession of another clue, thanks almost entirely to my dad. I handed the vendor seven bucks (I would have gladly paid $700) and left the Tri-County Flea Market with a heaping dose of

The flea market photo. Moments after the home run clears the wall, Andy Pafko stands in disbelief as the Giants fans shower the field with confetti. *From the author's collection*

renewed hope and my dad at my side. With two key photographs showing the place where the ball landed from two different angles, I felt better equipped to take my CSI approach.

Because I grew up in the blue-collar neighborhood of Howard Beach, Queens, I knew a lot of kids whose dads were New York City cops. I hoped that through one of their contacts I could get a detective on board to start analyzing the photo, pixel by pixel. None of those leads panned out. But from making a few calls, I realized that the Special Forensic Unit was where I needed to find my expert, and I remembered another way to get there.

Susan Watts was a photojournalist who had a dozen years' experience working for the *New York Daily News.* I had met her several years back when she was on assignment taking pictures at the dog run in Carl Schurz Park at East Eighty-fifth Street. I was there with Mike, my brown schnauzer, and we became fast friends because we are both animal lovers. And we've stayed friends ever since. Since cops and photographers are often in the same places at the same times during crime-scene investigations, Susan knew everyone who was anyone in that world. She was kind enough to open up her Black-Berry to me.

The first guy I contacted was Dan Austin, a decorated forensic detective who had recently retired from the NYPD. I did my homework on him, and I was impressed. Daniel C. Austin Jr. is a third-generation New York City police officer. He entered the Detective Bureau in 1994 and was assigned to the Forensic Investigations Division's Crime Scene Unit. He was thrust into the public spotlight his first year when he was in charge of forensic reconstruction in the infamous Queens Boulevard Christmas shootout at Tung Shing House in Rego Park, Queens, New York. Congressman Gary Ackerman and his wife were nearly killed while dining in the popular Chinese eatery. Others weren't so lucky. In the end, three people were murdered and two police officers wounded. Austin performed a ballistics reconstruction that placed the perpetrators at the scene and identified them by their shell casings. Shortly after this headline-grabbing incident, the Emmy Award–winning TV show *NYPD Blue* produced an episode about this very crime. Detective Austin also helped solve a thirty-year-old homicide on Staten Island by replicating photographs from the crime scene, he was the lead forensic investigator in a fatal scaffolding collapse on Park Avenue, and he aided in the investigation of American Airlines Flight 587, which crashed in

Rockaway, Queens, in 2001. Austin has been designated an expert witness in over three hundred trials and has been called upon to testify over four hundred times.

When I spoke to him the first time, he said, "When you told me you were working on a project about the Shot Heard 'Round the World, at first I thought you were talking about the Revolutionary War. Then I mentioned it to a few friends and they immediately said, 'Bobby Thomson.' It's like everyone knew about this game."

As a history buff and baseball fan, he took to the project right away. I went to meet him at his office in Maspeth, Queens. He looked to be straight out of central casting, like a mustachioed David Caruso: a fit, redheaded guy with a New York accent. He wore a blue suit with an American flag pin on his lapel. Around the collar of his starched white shirt was a solid-red tie with a perfect Windsor knot. Austin spoke at length to me about his experience, how he had analyzed hundreds of crime scenes looking for the clue that another cop might have missed. His particular area of expertise was in photo analysis. He'd looked at over thirty thousand photos in his career. Within a minute, I knew this was my guy.

I showed him the photos.

"This is all I have. Is there *anything* you could do for me?"

He held up *Pafko at the Wall*.

"Well, this one is a little bit grainy, and there are a lot of different things happening in it."

The door to Austin's office opened, and a tall man in his late forties with a thick black mustache sprinkled with gray walked in. I knew immediately he was a cop—the .38 caliber Smith & Wesson revolver strapped to his belt was a dead giveaway.

"I asked one of my colleagues to join us. Brian, meet Henry Rogan."

Rogan was a detective a year short of retirement. He stepped into the room with his suit jacket flung over the shoulder of his light blue shirt.

"Henry, we have these two pictures, and that's it," Austin said. "You think there's anything we could do for this young man?"

"Let's take a look."

Rogan and Austin took a photo each and studied them carefully, holding magnifying glasses and various loupes to them. They passed the pictures back and forth several times comparing observations.

"I'd like to blow them up. Then we can really see what we have." Austin said.

"It'll be tough, because you run the risk of overpixelating them, but we could try," Rogan answered. After twenty minutes of watching the detectives flesh out every minor aspect of the pictures, I saw Austin's impressive observational skills in action. When *Pafko at the Wall* originally ran in the newspaper back in 1951, an editor had placed an arrow pointing toward a man in the front row, implying that this was the guy who caught the ball. But it didn't make any sense. If this guy had indeed caught the baseball and then had his picture in the paper, there wouldn't be any mystery to solve. At some point, he would have come forward with this picture as proof that he was the guy with the ball. Sure enough, before long, Detective Austin said, "I don't know what this arrow is doing here. It was probably presumed that he caught the ball because he looks so animated, but I can tell you right now that he didn't."

"How do you know that for sure?"

Leaning forward, Austin pointed out something I had never realized. "Look at the eyes of everyone in the photo. If the guy with the arrow caught it, why would all these people be looking back, over their shoulders, and not directly at him?"

The eyes of the other people in the picture *were* looking back—toward an area in the fourth or fifth row. Austin then pointed out another interesting thing.

"Henry, look at this mass in front of the guy with his arms up and mouth open."

"Yeah, I see that. What do you suppose that is?"

"I'm not really sure. Could it be an old paperboy cap he pulled off his head to try and catch the ball?"

Henry leaned in, and together he and Austin stared down at the picture.

"Wait. You know what? I think that's a mitt on his left hand," Austin said enthusiastically.

Rogan was squinting at the photo, totally focused. After a moment, he agreed that the man was wearing a baseball glove on his left hand.

"Hold on. Look at that! You see that white dot, Dan? Do you suppose that could be the baseball inside the mitt?"

My heart raced. Two men I had just met were about to solve the greatest mystery in sports in my presence. Austin stood up and pumped his fist as Rogan and I looked on, grinning at each other.

"Brian, I'm not making you any promises, but I feel we have a solid lead here. I'd like to hold on to the pictures and maybe bring in another photography expert to do an extensive analysis. There's so much new technology."

I left Austin's office that day feeling reborn. Less than a year ago, I'd been so disabled by mental illness that I barely had the ability to interact with anyone other than my own family, and now I was sitting with two decorated crime-scene detectives telling me there was a chance I might be able to resolve the sports equivalent of "Rosebud."

By tracing the sight lines of the fans, detectives Dan Austin and Hal Sherman were able to determine exactly where the baseball landed. The man with the white arrow pointed at him did not catch it. *Modified from Hank Olen's* Pafko at the Wall, *courtesy of Patrick McCarthy*

Austin said he would contact a man named Pat McCarthy, a brilliant photo analyst with the instincts of a top detective, who was also a photographer with *New York Newsday,* and we would all get together in a few weeks.

As good as I was feeling, I wasn't content with just one team of forensic experts working on the case. Through Susan I contacted Hal Sherman, a former detective first grade, and a specialist on recovering physical evidence. Both Sherman and Austin had worked as crime-scene investigators at division headquarters, located at 150-14 Jamaica Avenue, Queens. They'd crossed paths several times over a ten-year period but never actually worked a case together. Detective Sherman is a forensic consultant for the NYPD, and was a lead investigator in both World Trade Center attacks. He also had been a consultant on films like *The Bone Collector* and *Summer of Sam,* so I thought he'd be willing to help me with my movie. Sherman's style is old-school cop mixed with new-school technology. He invited me to Taka Labs, a mini CSI facility he set up with his partner, Tom Kubic, in East Northport, Long Island.

I took the hour-long drive to the northern tip of Long Island with my production crew to meet Sherman. He was dressed in a lab coat with a shirt and tie underneath. A polite guy with an understated wit, Detective Sherman was thorough in his questioning and methodology after I showed him the two photos Austin had seen. Rubbing his neatly trimmed, graying goatee, he noticed Pafko's body position first. The *Daily News* picture was slightly different from the flea market one—the same observation I had made when first seeing it at Tri-County. After several anxious moments of silence—with Sherman peering down at the photos through his sleek, square eyeglasses—he revealed his initial finding. Then Detective Sherman wedged the *Daily News* photo between two stage clips on a microscope wired to a TV monitor so we all could see exactly what he was seeing. After several more moments of disconcerting silence, he suddenly popped his head up.

Sherman had come to the same conclusion as detectives Austin and Rogan—the eyes of the fans in section 35 were directed a few rows behind the man with the arrow. Then Sherman pointed to a specific fan in the front row dressed in a gray flannel jacket with a cigarette dangling from his mouth whose head was turned completely around, looking over his left shoulder at what was behind him. It was obvious that if the man with the arrow had caught the ball, this person would be looking across, not back.

To support his eye-line theory, Detective Sherman also performed a blood spatter demonstration, a technique often used in crime-scene investigations to determine the direction a bullet enters a victim's body. Standing upright, he squirted a drop of blood from a plastic tube onto the ground. Then he examined it through a magnifying glass, pointing out how the blood spatters out in many different directions on impact, forming a sunburst effect. But when you follow each line of the sunburst, they all trace back toward one point—the center. He compared the blood spatter to the eyes of the people in the photograph—all leading back toward one particular spot in the left-field stands. That's where he believed the ball landed. And it was right near the guy Austin said was wearing a mitt.

OK, so now we knew for sure that the guy with the arrow wasn't relevant. Then where did the ball go? I didn't tell Sherman what Austin had concluded because I wanted to see if he would determine that the man with his mouth open and arms up was indeed wearing a baseball mitt. I grew anxious when he didn't, especially because he was using a high-power microscope. But after he concluded that the ball had landed three to five rows back, at least I had both forensic teams agreeing on something. Before leaving Taka Labs, I asked Sherman what he thought my best bet would be for finding the actual baseball. He told me the answers were in the photos, most likely *Pafko at the Wall.* He said he would conduct a grid search on the famous picture. It's another technique used in searching for evidence. The trained eye scans up and down and back and forth, looking at every detail for clues. He would get back to me with his final results.

What started as a small favor soon became a passionate project for the detectives. Sherman, Austin, and Rogan went to work on the photos with the same intensity they once showed while trying to solve murders on the streets of New York. It was the kind of thorough investigative work that no one had ever done in the world of sports, and they were excited to be a part of it. They put in dozens of hours of research and photo analysis to try to figure out the

Left: This image allowed Dan Austin and Hal Sherman to prove that the baseball, long believed to have been caught by the man in the black jacket and white T-shirt, is in midflight, not yet caught. *Right:* Using 3-D imaging, the baseball, an inanimate object *(circled),* stands out from the people in the crowd. *Modified from Hank Olen's* Pafko at the Wall, *courtesy of Patrick McCarthy*

truth about Thomson's baseball. They worked nights and weekends, and they called and e-mailed me dozens of times with questions. Austin also told me that he was in the process of obtaining a blueprint of the Polo Grounds through connections he had at the Parks Department. He had a theory that had something to do with the angle of the sun in *Pafko at the Wall.* I couldn't imagine what he was onto, but something told me it could be big.

The call I had been waiting for finally came. It was Dan Austin. I could tell right away from the excited tone of his voice that he and Henry Rogan had found something. I rushed to his Queens office. I hoped he would confirm that the white dot was the baseball and that we would be going on a manhunt for the suspect with the mitt.

Austin and Rogan introduced me to Pat McCarthy, a baby-faced man in his midforties. McCarthy had brought all his computer equipment to Austin's office and set it up like a mini evidence room.

The back of the Polo Grounds allowed sunlight to shine into the left-field stands. *Courtesy of the Michael Frank collection*

McCarthy began talking me through their scanned computer images of the photographs. They had made a remarkable discovery in *Pafko at the Wall*. McCarthy had converted the photo from a two-dimensional to a three-dimensional image using an advanced version of Photoshop. In the 3-D version, you could see the shapes of people's faces much more clearly, even their very expressions. In their analysis, they focused on the area where the man suspected to be wearing the mitt was standing. Right by this spot in the middle of the photo, you could see that in front of his face was a spherical object. It was the Thomson baseball! The actual ball floating in midair—not yet caught—among the grainy faces in the old black-and-white *Daily News* photograph snapped by Hank Olen. It had been hiding in plain sight all these years, blended in with the black-and-white faces in the picture. There was no doubt. McCarthy enlarged the photo on his

The Colonial Park housing project buildings reflected sunlight into the left-field seats. *Courtesy of the Michael Frank collection*

computer screen. Then Austin's team introduced a blueprint and an old photo of the Polo Grounds infrastructure. This was where Austin's theory about the sun, which he had hinted about to me on the phone, came into play. His team used the angle of the sun to confirm that the object was indeed the baseball. The sun was beginning to set behind the first-base side when the home run was hit at 3:58 P.M. It pointed down at a row of apartment buildings that lined Harlem River Drive on the other side of the stadium. Then its rays reflected off the apartments and back through the open end at the rear of the stadium at that time of day. This verified that the round object they located had sunlight on the top portion and a shaded bottom half, which was consistent with what would have happened on the baseball. This amazing discovery of a clear image of the ball everyone thought was lost forever was not just another small miracle—it was the big break I had been hoping for.

Hank Olen holds his Graflex camera, the same one used when snapping *Pafko at the Wall*. Courtesy of the *New York Daily News*

My Fifteen Minutes of Fame

Wednesday, October 3, 1951

Sal Marchiano was exactly ten years and seven months old. From the age of nine, he had been an obsessive Dodgers fan. He lived in the Carroll Gardens section of Brooklyn, a working-class Italian neighborhood. Marchiano attended Sacred Heart of St. Stephen, a Catholic school. That Wednesday, he decided to play hooky, and he watched the entire game by himself on the black-and-white TV set in his living room, wearing his Brooklyn Dodgers cap—blue with white lettering. He suffered through every inning, afraid in his heart of hearts that his team might lose, even when they took the lead. The long hallway in his apartment had a shiny parquet floor. To ease the tension, he put a throw pillow from the sofa at one end, and between innings, in his stocking feet, he practiced his sliding. His favorite maneuver was a hook slide, and as he did it, he always imagined eluding the tag of an imaginary shortstop, usually Alvin Dark of the Giants. As the game drew closer to the ninth inning, little Sal was getting more and more nervous, running up and down the long hallway like a lunatic. For a second, he actually believed the boys in blue would prevail—and he hoped that beating the Giants and going to the World Series would wipe away the terrible disappointment of the year before, when the Dodgers lost on the last day of the season to the Phillies. But it wasn't meant to be. *After the moment occurred, he just stared at the TV set, shocked that something so terrific could be taken away in an instant. He didn't have any time to mourn. He had an altar boy meeting to go to at four o'clock and was already late. He got up, and walked solemnly to the church a few blocks from his home. On the way over, he defiantly wore his Brooklyn Dodgers cap amid a handful of Giants fans running through the streets celebrating. Sure, the Dodgers had lost, but he wasn't about to abandon his team. There was always next year. And that loyalty stayed with him, almost to a fault. Years later, Marchiano described the eternal influence it had on him this way: "October third, 1951—a day of infamy in my life and for thousands of others. Bobby Thomson changed my world . . . he rocked my world. And it never goes away. To this day, I can't enjoy baseball. But because of my profession, I have to watch it."*

GROWING UP, *Vic Ziegel thought of himself as a pilgrim in an unholy land. He was a Giants fan living deep in the heart of Yankee country—Grant Avenue in the Bronx—a mere two subway stops from Yankee Stadium. He and his pal Harvey Koch were the only Giants fans in the neighborhood, as far as he knew. On the day of the big game, Ziegel was a fourteen-year-old attending Taft High School, a few blocks from his family's apartment building. He didn't bother asking his parents if he could stay home from school that day because he knew the answer would be no. Immigrants from Eastern Europe, they didn't share young Vic's passion for the American pastime. His dad had taken him to only one ball game in his life—an exhibition game between New York City police and firemen that took place at Yankee Stadium. Ziegel wasn't old enough to have seen his Giants win a pennant, and this game—the third and deciding game of a playoff for the National League pennant—meant the world to him. The Yankee fans in the neighborhood had tormented Vic for years, taunting him with their team's many successes. He was praying that in the World Series his Giants would finally give him a chance to shut them up.*

A year before, a classmate had snuck a small radio into class to hear his Yankees play in the fall classic. Vic was secretly hoping that someone would try that move again this year, but it wasn't meant to be. He had no such luck and knew he'd have to sweat it out until three o'clock. Even more than usual, the school-day minutes seemed like hours, until finally he heard the blissful sound of the bell signifying the end of classes. While it was still echoing in the halls, Ziegel flew out a side-door exit on 171st and Sheridan streets.

He sprinted home in his sneakers, the chest pocket of his polo shirt flapping in the breeze that blew across Grant Avenue. He got to his door at 1328 Grant and raced up three flights of stairs, breathing heavily by the time he got to the front door. When he pushed the metal door open, his mom was there, but she was not watching the game. Barely acknowledging her, Ziegel rushed into the living room and flung open the two white cabinet doors that encased his parents' brand-new Sentinel TV, their first. He turned the channel knob until he found the game, was relieved when he found it, then horrified to see that the Giants were down 4-1. But there were still three and a half innings left, so Vic hung on to some hope that his guys would come back.

Ziegel's mom saw how passionate her son was about the Giants and decided to watch the rest of the game with him. When the Dodgers manager, Charlie Dressen, pulled Don Newcombe for Ralph Branca in the ninth, Vic knew his team had a puncher's chance, as Thomson had a history of hitting the long ball against Branca. Thomson dug his spikes into the dirt, and two pitches later, Ziegel tasted euphoria. When his mom saw how excited he was, she clasped hands with him, and the two danced in a circle around the living room. And once he and his mom stopped celebrating, he decided to go outside to find Harvey Koch or anyone else to share his excitement with. But he couldn't find his buddy, and the rest of the streets were quiet. Ziegel expected at the very least to see Yankee fans out on their stoops marveling over the Thomson blast. After all, no matter whom you rooted for, it was just a remarkable end to an extraordinary game and season. Then it occurred to him—the result wasn't that big a deal to the Yankee fans in the neighborhood, *because they were used to winning. And Thomson or no Thomson, they certainly were not afraid of the weak sisters from the National League who hadn't won a championship in the previous eighteen years. Outside on those Bronx streets, Ziegel was a little disappointed that he hadn't found anyone with whom to enjoy the glory, but inside he was never so happy. To this day, he calls the Shot Heard 'Round the World the happiest moment of his life. He described the search for the missing artifact perfectly: "The Thomson ball is the Holy Grail, the Magna Carta, the Constitution. It's King Tut."*

HANK OLEN'S FAMOUS photograph *Pafko at the Wall* is a small miracle in and of itself, given the circumstances under which it was shot. Olen was seated 350 feet away, high above the field in the press box behind home plate, so he had no margin for error. The crafty lensman was using his clunky, black, oversize Graflex camera, and it wasn't as simple as pointing and clicking. Every new shot required changing the film sheet, focusing the camera, cocking the shutter, and pressing the shutter after each exposure. It's amazing that in one click he was able to capture the baseball itself the very instant it floated into the stands. Olen had to anticipate exactly when to pull the trigger, because if he missed it, he wouldn't have enough time to reload. His timing was perfect, and his picture remains one of the most famous in sports history.

Austin and Sherman's findings allowed me to narrow down the suspects to those seated closest to the ball—approximately a half dozen people. Since the game happened more than fifty years ago and the people in the relevant area were all adults, I didn't think there would be much chance that any were still alive. My best hope was that a relative or neighbor might recognize one of them. But how could I get tens of thousands of people in New York to see this photo? I asked Detective Sherman for his opinion. He told me about a famous case from 1993.

State police in Somers, New York, had tried in vain for years to identify a body found in the Titicus Reservoir. The only clue they had was an old photograph they found on the John Doe's body floating in the water, which showed an elderly man holding a little boy. The picture appeared to have been taken in the late fifties or early sixties. Even after analyzing every detail of the photo, they still couldn't make a positive ID on the location, let alone the body.

Years passed, and the police finally agreed to run the picture in the newspaper. Sure enough, a woman saw the picture and recognized a building in the background. This information was crucial to the troopers. With it, they identified the dead body found thirteen years earlier and finally solved the case.

"So you think if I get what I've found printed in the New York papers, someone might come forward?"

"In a city like New York, you'd get a ton of responses if the picture ran with a story or maybe if there were a piece on the news." Sherman had a final word of warning though: "Just be prepared. The crazies could come knocking at your door."

First on my hit list was Vic Ziegel. He had written extensively about the Thomson ball, and while he could be a bit cynical at times, I wanted him in my corner. After talking to Ziegel on the phone, I was able to schedule a meeting for a few days later with him and the top sports editors at the *Daily News*.

I told my dad the good news, and he joked that I should tell Ziegel to write a *positive* article about him this time. I was eager to make my case at the *Daily News* and counted down the days to the meeting like a prizefighter waiting to step into the ring for a championship fight. All of my photographic evidence was stored in a small cabinet behind the reception desk at Tangerine Films. On the day of the meeting, I gathered up all the photos, walked out of the West Twenty-seventh Street office, and headed northeast to the gigantic skyscraper where the *Daily News* offices are housed. Crossing Eighth Avenue right by Madison Square Garden, I took a mental inventory of the large white cardboard envelope I was carrying under my arm. There was a super-size version of *Pafko at the Wall* with a dotted white circle around the ball, a three-dimensional rendition of the picture, and another version of the picture with white lines inserted to trace the fans' sight lines directly to the baseball.

I was given a visitor's pass up to the third floor of the building. The security guard escorted me to a seating area that faced two glass doors leading into the newsroom. From where I was seated, I could see a Plexiglas display case with several artifacts from the paper's history, including the type of camera Olen used to snap *Pafko at the Wall*. This was a good omen, and suddenly I knew the meeting was going to go well. My goal was simple: Persuade the *Daily News* to write an article, including a blown-up version of the photograph, to see if any of the paper's 750,000 readers would recognize a face in the crowd.

As I walked through the hallway toward the newsroom, I was so taken by the artwork lining the white walls that I got lost in the moment and nearly forgot why I was there. Numerous oversize front and back newspaper pages were displayed like a time line of American history: papers marking the end of World War II; little John-John giving his famous last salute to his dad; the 1969 moon landing; and Mark Messier, the New York Rangers center, hoisting the 1994 Stanley Cup.

I made my way into a conference room with Ziegel, editor Teri Thompson, assistant sports editor Adam Berkowitz, and columnists T. J. Quinn and Michael O'Keeffe. O'Keeffe worked on what was called the sports investigative team, and I was familiar with his work and happy to see him in the room. As much as Ziegel was an appropriate choice to write about my search because of his New York Giants connections, this story was even more of O'Keeffe's bailiwick. When O'Keeffe started at the paper in 1998, he had quickly gained fame, breaking a flurry of stories about the reappearance of five baseballs stolen from the Hall of Fame in the 1970s. And he and Thompson were currently collaborating on a book about the incredibly rare Honus Wagner T-206 baseball card from 1909. That particular baseball card, which was inserted inside cigarette packs in the early 1900s, was the *Mona Lisa* of baseball cards. Thompson and O'Keeffe had an appreciation for antique sports pictures and valuable artifacts that most others didn't.

As the group exchanged pleasantries and talked about the previous night's Yankees game, I reached into my large cardboard envelope and got everyone's attention. I pulled out my *Pafko at the Wall* print, which immediately caught the eyes of Thompson and O'Keeffe. I asked everyone why they thought the arrow pointed at the man in the front row. Ziegel quickly told me, "An editor must have put it there the day after the game to indicate he caught the ball . . . or maybe that's where it landed."

I asked him to closely examine the photo. He slightly squinted his eyes, holding them for a few beats on the picture.

"What am I supposed to be looking for?"

"The ball, Vic."

"I don't understand."

Then, as everyone's attention was focused squarely on me, I explained the eye-line discovery my detectives had made. Vic stared back down at the picture. He pursed his lips and passed it on to Thompson. While she examined it, I pulled out the version with the white lines.

"Look at the lines. These were inserted by detectives who solve murders. According to them, if the man with the arrow had the ball, the focus of all these fans would be on him. But notice where they're looking."

"So why do you think the arrow is there?" Ziegel asked me.

"The editor in 1951 made a mistake," I explained to the group. "The arrow fan looks very animated, his arms are raised like he caught the ball—only he didn't catch the ball."

No one responded except Thompson, "How can you be so sure?"

"Because now I am going to show you exactly where the ball is."

Ziegel inched forward in his seat. Holding the picture with the circle around the ball, I said, "The Thomson ball couldn't have been caught by the man with the arrow because it's actually still floating in midair!" I pointed my finger directly at the spot and said the words I had been waiting to say for the last six months: "It's right *there*."

Everyone wanted to be the first to see it. One by one they leaned forward in their chairs and stared down at the picture that I had now placed on a desk.

Adam Berkowitz bolted out of the room as I went on to explain that, according to the forensic experts, the reason it was shaded was that the sun was actually coming in through the back end of the stadium, lighting the top half and keeping the bottom part dark.

The reaction in the room was enthusiastic. I could tell that I had delivered something big and that the *Daily News* crew thought they were sitting on a groundbreaking story. Thompson asked me a ton of questions about the background of the detectives who'd helped me, and after I supplied a brief bio of Austin and Sherman, she turned to Ziegel.

"What can I say? I can't argue with the cops."

Suddenly Berkowitz flew back into the room with a paper printout of *Pafko at the Wall* that he'd got from the art department. He must have blown it up 500 percent. "He's right," said Berkowitz. "That's the ball."

"It's been there all these years and nobody knew it," O'Keeffe said with amazement. "This is a major breakthrough."

I told them that this photo, accompanied by a story asking for readers' help, could provide us with the information needed to unearth the most famous baseball never found. Thompson agreed immediately, and O'Keeffe chimed in, "I mean, where has the ball been for the last fifty years? Someone has to know, right?"

The *Daily News* was onboard. O'Keeffe would report the story, with Ziegel adding a sidebar. The only questions now were when would it appear and how much space would it get?

I pushed for the back cover.

GETTING A MAJOR newspaper to print the photo of our "suspects" was a big deal for me. Still, I felt if I could get the two other media, TV and radio, involved, I would have no excuses if failure came my way. If having the word spread all across the New York tristate area couldn't yield success, then perhaps the mystery would never be solved, or maybe I just wasn't the guy to solve it. But I was going to give it everything I had. By this point in the process, my desire began taking over my life. I had come so far in getting my life back on track. As I inched closer to solving this riddle, I was also moving away from that dark time of hopelessnes and fear, so that every day now felt like a gift.

When I initially spoke with Sal Marchiano, I told him how much my dad loved the Brooklyn Dodgers. According to Sal, it was *he,* not my dad, who was the biggest Brooklyn Dodgers fan on the planet. This was one of the first things he said to me when we met: "In Brooklyn in those days, you had the holy trinity . . . God, family, and the Brooklyn Dodgers."

Fresh from my successful meeting at the *Daily News,* I had a

7:00 P.M. appointment with Marchiano at the WB11 (WPIX) studios on East Forty-second Street. If I could convince a whole team of skeptical print reporters, I was sure to have a good chance with an amiable sports anchor I'd already befriended. Sal Marchiano is to New York sports what Jackie Mason or Jerry Seinfeld is to comedy. He's a native New Yorker, and he always comes across like "one of the guys."

As I entered Marchiano's office, he was talking on the phone, so I had a minute to examine the impressive exhibit of autographed photos on his walls. There was a framed photo of him interviewing Mickey Mantle in the 1960s, another beauty with Willie Mays, and yet another classic with Broadway Joe Namath.

Sal wrapped up his call, and we sat and chatted for a few minutes about how I had formed a team of forensic detectives who examined *Pafko at the Wall* in ways no one had ever done before. Sal took it all in but stayed noncommittal. Part of him must have thought that I was just another kook. Then I reached down to my trusty white cardboard envelope.

I slid the original *Pafko at the Wall* onto his desk. Marchiano was immediately back in that moment that broke his heart as a little boy.

"Ah, geez. Look at him . . . Andy Pafko . . . he didn't have a chance," Marchiano lamented. "It was a sinking line drive. Any other ballpark would have held it, but not the Polo Grounds. . . ." Marchiano's voice trailed off.

I took Marchiano through all the photographic evidence, and he grew more intrigued by the moment. His shock, disbelief, and enthusiasm that the ball could be seen in the picture prompted him to ask me who else I had shared this information with. I told him that other than the *Daily News,* no other media outlet was privy to it. His face lit up. He wanted the exclusive for broadcast.

"What did you have in mind?" he asked.

I wasn't exactly sure what I wanted, but I explained that by broadcasting the photograph, especially the blown-up section where the suspects were, maybe we could get people to come forward with information that might lead to our actually finding the ball. I told him I wanted to set up an 800 number to help sift through all the responses.

"You're right. Someone could be sitting on this million-dollar ball and not even know it. Their father or grandfather could have passed it down to them, and because they don't know its true value, they've never stepped forward."

I reminded him that most people don't even know it's missing.

"True. I didn't know, but then again I'm not into collecting memorabilia."

"That's the whole point, Sal. In those days, nobody was. It might be sitting up in a shoebox in someone's closet, and they have no clue what they're in possession of."

"This is a fantastic story. I want to do a feature. I'd like to get you on camera explaining all of this, and we'll cut together a piece about the missing ball. I love this kind of stuff."

Before walking me out, Marchiano introduced me to some of the other producers and broadcasters he worked with. I was particularly interested in talking with Lolita Lopez. She was the weekend sports anchor, and she covered the Mets beat closely. Little did I know that Lopez would reappear with a piece of knowledge a few months later that would play a large role in solving the mystery.

Both media outlets wanted to be the first to break the story, which caused a minor conflict, but they worked out an agreement. The *Daily News*—whose picture it was in the first place—would print their story first, and Marchiano would air a feature the next night on "Sal's Sports," a special segment of his show geared toward features and human-interest stories.

When the four-page story ran in the *Daily News* on Sunday, June 4, 2006, the back of the paper had a blue banner headline that read: CSI POLO GROUNDS—DAILY NEWS GOES BEHIND SCENES OF FASCINATING NEW EVIDENCE IN SEARCH FOR BOBBY THOMSON'S LONG-LOST HOME RUN BALL.

It wasn't exactly the entire back-page coverage I had hoped for, but at least I got my back-page headline. The feature was one of the largest non-news stories ever published in the history of the paper. (It rivaled a six-page spread written in 2004 by Wayne Coffey about the tragic plane crash that took the life of famous Yankees catcher Thurman Munson on August 2, 1979.)

A few days before the Sunday story hit the newsstands, I was invited up to the WB11 studio to tape my interview with Marchiano. My photojournalist friend Susan accompanied me because I had never been on TV before and needed a little confidence booster. Besides, her apartment was only a short walk from the studio on East Forty-second Street, and she thought it would be cool to watch. She reminded me about something that I had recently learned firsthand by interviewing others for my documentary.

"Remember to let him finish his question before responding," she said, while adjusting the collar of my shirt, which stubbornly didn't want to sit right, inside my sport jacket. "I'm sure you already know how difficult it is to edit an interview when someone is stepping on your lines, right?"

After so many months being on the other side of the camera, it felt a little awkward at first, but Marchiano was an old pro at keeping his subjects relaxed, and I found my poise and rhythm quickly.

After we finished, I thanked him profusely for his help and also told him how much his fellow Dodgers fan Jack Biegel appreciated it. In return, he gave me his cell-phone number and told me to call him if I ever got any solid leads on the ball. The old pro was already planning for a follow-up piece. That was sweet music to my ears.

Susan and I left the studio and blended in with the scores of other New Yorkers walking up and down the streets of Manhattan. But something was different about me. I thought about how far I'd come in the last nine months. To go from near self-destruction to having my name and face all over the New York media—for all the right reasons—gave me a euphoric sense of freedom. I'd been on the bottom and was headed back toward the top. It was all a bit surreal but comforting at the same time.

A few nights later, I asked my dad to record the ten-o'clock Marchiano broadcast for me. I was going to be in the edit room late and didn't know if I'd make it home in time to watch it live. As excited as I was about seeing myself on TV, my first priority was still making sure everything was in order with my film. When I pulled my car into the driveway, it was close to midnight. I noticed the lights in the living room were still on. I opened the front door and immediately saw my mom sitting on the couch with a rolled-up tissue in her hand. The broadcast had ended over an hour ago, but she and Dad had stayed up to greet me.

As Mom got up from the couch to approach me, she began talking but couldn't hold back her tears.

"We're so proud of you, Brian. You've come so far, and that is what makes us the happiest. Seeing you feeling better, being your old self, is all we ever want to see."

My dad was trying to play it cool, but I could see right through his tough veneer.

"You looked good, kid. Was that my shirt you were wearing?" Dad said, smirking.

"Poppa, you could buy five Gap shirts for the price I paid for that bad boy."

The three of us sat down in the kitchen. Dad and I spooned down a pint of chocolate fudge brownie ice cream while I asked them about every detail of my big TV appearance.

"So what did Marchiano say?"

"My favorite part was when he compared the ball to the Maltese Falcon," Dad answered.

"That's a great analogy. I love it! What else did he say? Did he show all the pictures and run the 800 number?"

"Brian, you were just fantastic," Mom said with her eyes gleaming. "The whole report was. He was on for almost three minutes. Then he had a little discussion with the news anchors. You're going to get hundreds of people swearing up and down that they have the ball."

Dad's eyes popped wide open and he turned to his wife. "Hey, how could they have it, *when I have it!*"

My dad was never a man to give up easily. I just tried to humor him. "We'll see, Poppa. We'll see."

Junk from the Attic

I t took only thirteen minutes for the first phone call to come in. But because of a technical glitch, I wasn't able to listen to any of the dozens of messages until two days after the *New York Daily News* story ran. As it turned out, I wasn't missing anything too important—unless you consider people trying to sell me junk from their attics important.

The first call was from a woman whose low-pitched voice and slow enunciation indicated she had probably been drawing a Social Security check for some years. "I don't have the ball but I have a 78 rpm record from 1951 of Russ Hodges singing 'The Giants Win the Pennant.' Are you interested in buying that record?"

A guy trying to sell me a baseball hit by Yogi Berros followed that. Not Berra, mind you. Berros.

Next in line was a man from Bayonne, New Jersey, who had a big problem with the fact that the *Daily News* made a mistake in their photo spread. There was a picture of Bobby Thomson running off the field, dodging the crowd that was trying to celebrate with their new hero. The caller took umbrage over the fact that it was actually Alvin Dark, not Bobby Thomson, in the picture. "You made a mistake on that picture there. No one knows baseball like me. The picture's wrong. Check your facts, pal."

The strange calls kept rolling in one after the other, and as Hal Sherman had predicted, many were from amateur con artists trying to cash in on the biggest prize in the memorabilia market. I was invited to appear on a live talk show on SNY-TV with Michael O'Keeffe. The word about the hunt for the missing ball was spreading around New York, and other media outlets wanted a piece of the action.

Walking out of makeup, I crossed paths with a very large man dressed in a dark pinstripe suit that looked as though it cost the same as a new Lexus. He was Carl Banks, former New York Giants linebacker and a member of the NFL's eighties all-decade team. Banks was the other guest on the show that night, rounding out the panel. And that's when it hit me—I was going on live TV! I was intimidated by the idea. I had never been on TV at all until a few nights earlier, let alone live TV, with hundreds of thousands people watching. But I knew I had to do it to help get the word out about my search.

Gary Apple, the host of *Daily News Live,* didn't prep me much, other than to tell me that I would have to explain the significance of the photos and maybe tell the story of how I got started on my search. As with the Marchiano appearance, I got in the zone once I got through the first few jittery moments. About two minutes into the segment, Banks asked me how I would try to authenticate the ball. I started to run down the checklist. "It would have to be a ball manufactured by Spalding with a Ford Frick stamp. Ideally, we'd want a ticket stub from section 35, maybe an old photo of a person that matched a fan near the ball in *Pafko at the Wall,* and we'd want to do forensic testing on the cowhide, proving it was a baseball from close to 1951. . . ."

But before I could finish, we had to cut to commercial. The producer then told Apple it was time to wrap the segment. Apple called my search for the Thomson ball "a fascinating story that we'll all keep an eye on," reading aloud the 800 number for the audience (it was also posted on the bottom of the screen), and then he thanked me for appearing on the show.

It was six P.M. when I left the Midtown studio on West Fifty-second Street, and I rushed back to the office to listen to more calls on the voice mail. I was hoping in vain that I might hear something from someone with actual information, not just some quack trying to sell me a spaldeen that his dad used in a stickball game played near the Polo Grounds in 1951.

I had asked one of the producers on the documentary, Rob Farber, and my assistant producer, Brendan Kahn, to sift through the calls in my absence. Brendan had been a real ally to me from the time I started making the film. We had become close friends. He was an invaluable part of my creative team and managed to help me out during his various breaks from the University of Miami, where he was about to graduate. When I got to the office that evening, he and Rob were there. They clearly wanted my attention from the second I walked through the door.

Brendan told me, "Brian, you're going to want to hear this."

"What? You got something? Let me hear it."

Rob played the message on speakerphone. A woman named Irene said she had Bobby Thomson's baseball. The office was empty except for the three of us. We all stared at each other, shocked. The woman said it with such nonchalance, I couldn't make heads or tails of it. I dialed her number thinking maybe her dad had been at the game and gave her the ball, or maybe she was some distant relative of Thomson's. The phone just rang and rang until her answering machine picked up. I left word for her to call me immediately.

Meanwhile, I listened to a few other messages, none of which seemed too significant. One was from a man named Irving who spoke with a raspy smoker's voice. Like the guy from Bayonne, Irving called to make a correction to a play described by Michael O'Keeffe in the newspaper. Irving claimed that the double Whitey Lockman hit before Thomson stepped up to bat was actually hit down the *right*-field line, not the left-field line. He was wrong about this—O'Keeffe's account of the play was correct—but I liked Irving anyway. Unlike the abrasive tone of Mr. Bayonne, Irving just sounded like a huge baseball fan who wanted to help. He spoke softly and sincerely, with an accent that reminded me of my grandfather. He mentioned that he was at the game, sitting in foul territory—just a few sections from where Thomson smacked the home run. Even if he didn't have any relevant information about the ball, I knew it certainly couldn't hurt to have a connection to a person who'd been fortunate enough to witness the event from such close range.

The next day around noon, Brendan came running to tell me that Irene called back and was on hold. I told him to get her number and I'd call her back from the edit room where I was working. My blood was curdling with anticipation. He hurried back with her number written on a yellow Post-it, and I said, "You call her. I'm too nervous."

"For real?" he asked.

"No. Not for real.... Give me that thing!"

I dialed the number. After the first ring, a woman answered the phone.

Brendan looked on as I listened to her story. She told me she'd been a baseball fan for a long time and that her dad used to take her to games frequently. Brendan's eyes were locked on me, trying to gauge my reactions as she spoke. After about thirty seconds of not knowing what she was saying, he leaned his head in toward the phone, trying to listen through the earpiece.

Then I heard the voice on the other end of the line say, "My dad gave me the ball when I was just a teenager."

"That's great. Now how do you know that your ball is the actual one?"

Brendan tried to high-five me, but I shooed him away, wanting to make sure I heard every detail.

Lo and behold, she was right—in a sense. She did have *a* Thomson ball—one from 1946. Her father caught the first home run Bobby Thomson ever hit, on September 18, 1946, off Bob Chipman of the Chicago Cubs at the Polo Grounds. He gave it to her before he died, and now she wanted to cash in on the big prize. She didn't understand that there was a difference between her ball and the one that disappeared in 1951. The Shot Heard 'Round the World this was not.

After the call, I confided in Brendan that I wasn't sure if I was ever going to actually find the ball and complete my mission. The emotional highs from the flurry of local media coverage mixed with the disappointing phone messages left me feeling confused. I still felt I was close to unraveling the mystery, but I knew I needed another miracle to help me find the truth. It was all beginning to take a toll, though. I could sense that my dad was itching for me to try to prove that the ball in the photograph was the same one he had, even though I thought I had already proved that his ball couldn't be the one because Thomson himself told me that he never signed the ball. But now that there had been this media blitz and there was still no ball, my dad's wheels were spinning. He told me one night on the phone, after I gave him an update, "If no one is coming forward with proof they were seated in section 35, why couldn't the person who *did* have it all these years be the same person who unknowingly donated it to the Salvation Army thrift shop in 1990?"

I didn't really have an answer for him. There was a small chance he really did have the ball after all. Hearing all these far-fetched stories on the voice mail made me feel a lot of sympathy for him. Perhaps I had closed him out too soon. This mission had lifted me out of a life of mental agony. And I owed that all to him. Part of me wanted to believe more than ever that his baseball was indeed the real Thomson ball, hiding right under my nose, the same way it was once hidden in *Pafko at the Wall*.

Brendan told me that there was another message I should probably listen to. It was from a strange-sounding man named Phil Simkins, who promised he could help us. According to Simkins, a self-proclaimed genius and inventor, he had a revolutionary way to see objects appear in photographs as though they were sitting directly in front of your face. Simkins insisted I must meet with him so he could demonstrate his latest contraption, the Teletron, a concave mirror that was supposed to help one see images in 3-D, and he went on to tell me that I'd never solve the mystery if I didn't hire him. We already had 3-D versions of the photos thanks to the forensic team, so I didn't quite understand why he was so sure we needed his invention. Simkins was persistent, though, and left several detailed messages about his other works. I admired his moxie. He seemed eccentric, but what was wrong with that? I was intrigued by Simkins, so I called him back and asked him about his credentials. He told me that he was a graduate of the Rochester Institute of Technology. I asked about his other work, and he told me that in 1997 he had a meeting with the New York Yankees' executive vice president and general counsel, David Sussman, to present another invention, the Kool Rope. He explained it to me on the phone as a rubber tube you take out of the freezer and wear as a "personal air conditioner" on sweltering hot days.

"The tube can be molded to your body, around the neck and under the arms, to keep you cool for up to one hour."

The idea seemed strange to me, and I wondered how Simkins had ever secured a meeting with the Yankees in the first place.

"What did they say to you after your presentation?"

"They just sent me a letter," he said in a professorial voice. He then read it to me over the phone, as if he knew I was going to ask this question.

"'Thank you for presenting your "Kool Rope" device to the New York Yankees. Our trainer examined and tested your product and determined that the Yankees have no use for it.'"

It was pretty obvious at this point that Simkins was not exactly playing with a full deck, but sometimes genius is linked to eccentricity. He was a colorful character, and at the very least, I could use him for the film. I wasn't in any hurry to set up our meeting, but interviewing him was on my to-do list.

I still had plenty of calls to listen to. I couldn't imagine how they could get any worse. But they did. One guy wanted me to stop the Thomson project and make a film on a completely different subject. His recorded message: "Yo. I don't got the ball but that's all right. I got something more important. Knowledge. Why don't you make a film about the Bible? Let the world know that the so-called Negroes, Hindus, and Native American Indians are the true children of Israel. You got the power to do it, man. I seen you on TV. Just give me a ring, and we'll work out the details."

There was a message from a young boy who alerted me that his father had the ball and had built a shrine to it. He spoke in an Indian accent and made a point of saying that he would get into a great deal of trouble if his father knew he was contacting me. He left specific days and times for me to call him back so we could talk in private. "My dad says the world is not ready to see it," the boy proclaimed.

Another message was from a man who wanted to sell me a St. Louis Cardinals game-used ball from the early seventies. I have no idea why he thought this was relevant, but the next caller was even further afield. He sounded like Edward G. Robinson and had a collection of Lionel trains with a freight car. The train had a piece of masking tape on top that had been signed by the 1970s Yankees pitcher Ed Figueroa. I was promised a good deal on it.

I was feeling too frustrated to listen anymore, so I asked Brendan to just let me know if anything worthwhile rolled in. I began feeling that I had failed somehow. Here I was on the heels of this major discovery, and these people were trying to sell me items you'd find at a low-end garage sale. I felt less like the sports version of Indiana Jones and more like some two-bit memorabilia dealer.

A couple of days later, I was sitting at my desk when a man walked in and headed straight for our receptionist, Kate. I assumed he was a messenger. He was dressed in baggy jeans, with a large satchel hanging from his shoulder that appeared to be filled with packages.

Kate came over to my desk and told me that Phil Simkins was here to see me.

Unlike so many of the skeptics who dismissed my own wild notions out of hand, I wasn't going to do the same to Simkins. I would hear what the man had to say. Simkins was a quirky-looking guy in his midfifties—six three with a wild mane of coarse reddish hair that stood upright like Cosmo Kramer's. I asked Kate to escort Simkins down the hall to the editing room at Heavy Light Digital.

The genius inventor of the Teletron had tracked me down through the company website and decided to just show up.

Hell-bent on proving to me that I'd need to hire him to solve the mystery, he was there to give me a firsthand look at what the Teletron could do.

When I entered the editing room to meet him, Simkins had already taken the Teletron out of his large bag and set it down on a desk. Next to it, he had a thick book of famous art opened to a picture of Leonardo da Vinci's *Last Supper*.

Speaking faster than the speed of light, Simkins began explaining to me how the Teletron could see objects in three-dimensional format. He reminded me of a poor-man's version of Doc Brown from *Back to the Future*.

"But we already had a forensic team study the photograph in 3-D, and that's how we know exactly where the ball is in the photo. Didn't you see the newspaper article?"

"Yes. Of course I saw the newspaper."

"Then I'm really unclear on how you can help me."

"There are other things that the Teletron does. Images appear in ways that you couldn't imagine."

"How many different ways could you see an image in 3-D?"

"Brian, you have to open up your mind. That's what the Teletron does. It allows you to see things that you never knew were there."

"But I know what's there. It's a baseball."

Simkins was rambling on so fast about his Teletron that I could barely stand to listen anymore. So to appease him I looked through this weird metal contraption at the picture I had seen a million times before.

"Well, you see anything?"

Now I was getting frustrated.

"Yeah, I see a blown-up version of the same picture I've been looking at for three months. And it's not even in 3-D like you said it would be."

Ignoring my words, he shifted the Teletron onto the da Vinci picture. After staring down at it for nearly a minute with the intensity of a tiger, he raised his head with the look of a madman.

"There. You see that?" Simkins said with a glazed look in his eyes. "Look straight at the picture through the Teletron . . . right where my finger is pointing."

Leaning down and looking through the Teletron, I saw nothing. Simkins swore that if I looked close enough, I'd see Simkins himself petting a billy goat, seated between various saints and apostles. I informed Mr. Simkins we would not need his services at this time.

The next day, I arrived early at the office, but Rob and Brendan were already there. I had talked to Brendan the previous night about Simkins and how I was nearing the end of my rope. But when I walked in, I immediately noticed an energized look on his face. He and Rob had just screened the previous night's calls, and there was one in particular they wanted to share.

"Oh, no. What now? Did Simkins spot himself sitting atop a unicorn on Noah's Ark?"

"Laugh all you want," Brendan said. "You're going to want to listen to this one."

The call came in very early in the morning. It was from a businessman named Norman Schimmel. I would later learn that Mr. Schimmel had several residences, including a home in Florida and a Manhattan apartment. He traveled all around the world on business and rarely spent time in New York—even though his roots were in Brooklyn. But he happened to be in New York City the day the article appeared in the *Daily News*.

Schimmel's voice sounded serious and legitimate. He explained that as an avid reader and even bigger baseball fan, he remembered reading the name of the fan who caught the Thomson ball in an old book called *Dodger Daze and Knights* from 1952 written by sportswriter

Tommy Holmes—who also had been the Dodgers beat reporter for the *Brooklyn Daily Eagle* newspaper.

Mr. Schimmel said, "I have every book ever written on the Brooklyn Dodgers and have never stopped following them. But in this book, which I'm assuming nobody even remembers, Tommy Holmes wrote somewhere that the ball was caught by a woman named Helen Fawn."

Schimmel spelled the name out letter by letter, "H-E-L-E-N F-A-W-N," and then left his contact information. I made my way to my computer, hoping to find another reference to this Helen Fawn. The first site to pop up raised my hopes briefly. It was a book called *Liberating Women's History*. I was intrigued by the idea that a woman, not a man, caught the most famous home run in history. With all the bizarre twists and turns so far, why not one more? It seemed unlikely to me that Helen's accomplishment would be enough to enshrine her in an actual women's history book, but maybe it was. I clicked through to find that the reason for the match was that in the book's acknowledgment section, the first names Helen and Fawn were listed next to each other alongside Lois, Roslyn, Ginny, and Hermia. No luck there.

The other close call came in the Whitley County, Indiana, marriage registry. It showed that a certain Helen Fawn married Paul Welsheimer in 1925. However, that meant that in 1951 Helen's last name would have been Helen Welsheimer, and she presumably lived far away from the Polo Grounds.

I told Brendan about what I'd found. He pointed out that just because there was no mention of Helen Fawn on the Web didn't mean anything at all. Maybe she got married after the '51 game, or maybe she had passed away and there just wasn't any virtual record of her. Then he asked me the question I'd spend the next eight months trying to answer, "How are we going to find Helen Fawn?"

Lifelong Dodgers fan Norman Schimmel in Brooklyn, circa 1951.
From the author's collection

Dodger Daze

Wednesday, October 3, 1951

The day Thomson launched his home run into the Polo Grounds seats, Norman Schimmel was a ten-year-old rabid Dodgers fan living two blocks from Ebbets Field. He shared a bedroom with his two older brothers, Stanley, 23, and Jack, 21. Stanley, Jack, and Norman were each born in different parts of the city, and each rooted for a different team. Stanley lived and died with the Giants, and Jack, the black sheep of the family, was a Yankees fan.

School was not an option that day for Norman—none of the Schimmel boys, not even Jack, could imagine the idea of not seeing such an historic game live. They huddled around their Dumont in the bedroom, sitting on the edge of the bed for the whole nine innings. Stanley, who had seen his team beaten by the hated Dodgers throughout his teenage years, was sure they were sunk from the moment the Giants fell behind 4-1. Norman also thought the game was a fait accompli. After all, his guys were ahead three runs most of the game and had it in the bag. He was supremely confident in the way only a ten-year-old could be. At that point, he thought that the Dodgers would win a pennant every year.

When the ball streaked into section 35, little Norman fell to his knees and choked back the tears. Stanley pranced around the room, jumping so high it looked as though his head might hit the ceiling. He approached his crying brother, put a hand on his shoulder, and said with a deadpan voice, "Too bad, kid."

Norman Schimmel ran out the door to the PS 241 schoolyard, where he and his friends often played. Within minutes, there were twenty neighborhood kids, all Dodgers fans, gathered on the steps, sharing a collective cry in near silence.

Big brother Stanley passed away in 2001, and Norman eulogized him. He talked about the '51 game, joking about how happy and surprised he was that after that rocky day, the two remained lifelong best friends. At the end of the eulogy, he draped a Giants jersey, number 24 for Willie Mays, over Stanley's casket.

THE PHONE CALL from Norman Schimmel made me ecstatic. Not only did I have what sounded like a genuine lead, but also the link to Helen Fawn. Was she still alive? Where did she live? Did she still have the ball? I also wanted to talk to Schimmel as soon as possible to set up a time to film him and see what else he knew.

But there was one thing I wanted to do first. I wanted to see if I could find this woman—or any woman for that matter—in the photos. I reexamined *Pafko at the Wall*. As I expected, the people in the immediate area where the ball landed were all men, except one—a tall thin woman with short, dark hair. Her head clearly poked through a crowd of men of various ages. She appeared to be in her midthirties.

Schimmel was a difficult man to find. The first time I reached him, he wouldn't let me get a word in edgewise because he was rushing off to make a flight. The second time, he was in Hong Kong and was getting bad cell reception so he couldn't really hear me. Each call took about thirty seconds. He did manage to tell me that he was going to be in New York a week later, but his schedule was jam-packed. That's when I offered to send a car to pick him up at the airport so I could interview him on the drive back to his high-rise apartment on East Thirty-third Street.

In the week leading up to the meeting with Schimmel, I was in a great mood. I just couldn't believe my good fortune. I tried to be cautiously optimistic throughout my search, but now, for the first time, I really started to think I was going to discover the fate of the ball. I had a legitimate, unbiased person with nothing to gain for himself. How could he possibly remember Helen Fawn from an obscure book written fifty-four years ago? What were the odds of that?

A few days before I was scheduled to interview Schimmel, I decided to do a little background research about Tommy Holmes. I knew he was a famous sportswriter who had covered the Dodgers back in the day, but that's pretty much all I knew. I contacted Brad Horn, at the Baseball Hall of Fame, to see if he had any other information about the man and to see if maybe they had a copy of *Dodger Daze and Knights,* the title Schimmel had mentioned, in their vast baseball library. Brad told me that he knew that Holmes was the recipient of the prestigious J. G. Taylor Spink Award, which he received posthumously in 1979. The Spink Award honors a writer or writers "for meritorious contributions to baseball writing." The list of honorees includes baseball writing giants like Dick Young, Red Smith, and Damon Runyon. Holmes was a sportswriting pioneer and deserving winner of the honor.

It was crucial that I get my hands on *Dodger Daze and Knights.* That's when I got the news that gave me serious worry. The Hall of Fame had Holmes listed as the author of three books: *Baseball's Best, A Tale of Two Cities,* and one simply titled *The Dodgers.* I asked if the Hall had a record of a book called *Dodger Daze and Knights* written by someone other than Holmes—maybe Schimmel had remembered the wrong author. The Hall had no book listed under that title. I felt as if I'd been kicked in the stomach. *Dodger Daze and Knights* was nowhere on the list! I had a horrible thought: What if Norman Schimmel was really just a saner version of Simkins?

I tried to keep it together. Maybe Schimmel was still right and just remembered the title wrong, or maybe the book had been retitled at some point along the line or packaged as part of some larger collection.

Anthony DeRiso, my old friend from Howard Beach, volunteered to be our driver for the day I met Schimmel. Anthony drove me and a small film crew out to LaGuardia Airport in his new Dodge Caravan. Schimmel's plane arrived on time from Sarasota, Florida, and I waited in the baggage area to greet him. I easily picked him out of the arriving passengers from the description he'd given me on the phone. A well-dressed man in his midsixties, Mr. Schimmel was about five seven, with a medium build, Florida tan, and designer eyewear. He was the president of a home furnishing company, and spent much of his time out of the country visiting manufacturing warehouses and securing big business deals for his company.

It was immediately clear that he was not a wild-eyed, crazy-haired, fast-talker like Simkins. Of course, I couldn't discount the possibility that the memory of such a busy man was just plain wrong. Sometimes when I'm on a project, I can't remember to set my TiVo, let alone recall a fact from a book I read years ago.

As we walked and talked on our way to the car, I realized how unlikely it was that I'd met Schimmel at all. He told me he was in New York just one day for the entire month of June, and it happened to be the exact day that the *Daily News* article ran.

"The funny thing is," Schimmel said, "I don't usually read the

Daily News. I prefer the *New York Post.* But on that day, the bagel shop I get my coffee at was out of the Sunday *Post,* so I grabbed the *News* instead."

I wondered to myself if the same baseball gods that put Esther Daniels in the Hall of Fame that day had brought Schimmel to me as well. I figured I'd start off the conversation by talking to him about his love of the old Dodgers and baseball in general. I asked him what he thought about the Red Sox breaking their eighty-six-year World Series drought.

"I have to say, as insane of a Dodger fan as I am, my wife, Patti, is even crazier about the Red Sox. You can't imagine the battles we've had over the years. And since they won the series, we're in this ongoing debate about who would win if the '55 Dodgers played the '04 Red Sox," Schimmel said, laughing.

He went on to explain that his favorite time to read was on those long airplane rides to Hong Kong for business. Of particular interest to him was anything about the Brooklyn Dodgers. Anything he could find on the team would go straight into his collection.

Then it was time for the $64 million question: Who is Helen Fawn?

"Obviously, I saw the article concerning the hunt for the lost ball. And I read some names of people who perhaps might be the people who may have that ball. None of those names seemed familiar to me, but as I was reading about, a name popped into my head. Believe it or not, I remember a book that I read about fifty years ago called *Dodger Daze and Knights.* I read it the year after the Shot Heard 'Round the World took place. The author was Tommy Holmes, who was a great sportswriter for the *Brooklyn Daily Eagle,* and he said the ball was caught by a woman named Helen Fawn. I remember that vividly."

It all just seemed too easy. Was he some sort of con man?

"Norman, you're certain of this? I have to tell you, I called the Baseball Hall of Fame, and they had no record of a book by Tommy Holmes with that title."

"That's not right." Then, holding his hand in front of his face as though it were a page from a book, he confidently said, "Helen Fawn's in writing. It's there."

"And you're sure the book was written by Tommy Holmes and not by somebody else?"

"As sure as the Dodgers moved out of Brooklyn."

He definitely believed he was telling the truth. Either that or he was a better poker player than Doyle Brunson. I decided to play along to draw more out of Schimmel.

I asked Norman how a Hall of Fame sportswriter like Tommy Holmes could write a book revealing the name of the person who caught the most famous baseball in history and yet for half a century no one picked up on this. It didn't make any sense. It would be a part of Dodger lore.

He explained that when Tommy Holmes wrote the book, there was no Dodger lore. People lived and died with the Dodgers, but according to Schimmel, they didn't obsess over those kinds of details back then.

I asked him how he could remember all of this so well, when every other New York baseball fan had no idea what happened to the ball. He told me that it was such an important day for him and he was so brokenhearted about the game that the name stuck out in his mind—even fifty-five years later. He added that other fans must just not have his memory for details.

Still fearing there was some sort of elaborate con going on, I gently asked him how come he didn't come forward with this information sooner?

Schimmel confessed that if he'd known that the information was so valuable, he would have spoken up sooner.

"I never thought after all these years the ball would still be unclaimed," Schimmel said with a shrug. "Especially with all that's happened in the memorabilia world. Didn't one of Mark McGwire's home-run balls sell for three million dollars?"

As much as I wanted to believe Schimmel, I still had questions. Why wouldn't the Hall know about the book? And even if Schimmel was right, why had neither Tommy Holmes nor *Dodger Daze and Knights* ever been mentioned before in connection with the Thomson ball? I tried to test Schimmel's memory a little more by asking him if he remembered anything else about Holmes.

"I remember hearing a story on the radio about how he ran up into the stands to try and find the person with the ball," he said calmly.

"Really? Do you think anyone else might remember this?"

"I thought you might ask me that. Before I left Florida, I called a few of my old Brooklyn pals to make sure I had all my facts straight. They remembered it the same way I did."

Schimmel explained that his old neighborhood buddies Barry Becher and Eddie Grad each remembered hearing a brief mention on WMCA radio about Tommy Holmes running toward the left-field stands, opposite the direction in which all the other reporters, cameramen, and fans were heading. They all were mobbing Thomson near home plate.

I knew from talking to the Logan boys that there was a stairway to the clubhouse in left center field. So this idea made sense: A reporter could have climbed up the stairs and hopped the rail to the outfield seats. From there, it seemed likely that other fans in the section could have pointed out where the ball landed, and he could have found the lucky fan. But Holmes would have had a long way to travel in a short time to get there, and he surely would have had a deadline to make. I didn't know what to think.

Anthony dropped us off in front of Mr. Schimmel's apartment building. He invited me up to his apartment for a cold drink and offered to show me his copy of *Dodger Daze and Knights*.

Schimmel hadn't mentioned in his initial message that he still had the book, but I was so excited that he did, I didn't ask any questions. In the elevator he asked, "How do you know so much about the Brooklyn Dodgers?"

"I'm just a fan, I guess, and they were my parents' favorite team."

"You couldn't imagine what it was like back then. Players lived right there in the same neighborhood with the fans. You'd go to buy a loaf of bread, and Gil Hodges would be standing in line in front of you."

I had to share my old man's story. "My dad used to deliver dry cleaning to the Duke."

Norm's face lit up. "I have a Duke Snider autographed bat up in the apartment! He was one of my all-time favorites."

The more time I spent with him, the more I liked him. Schimmel went to the bookshelves in his bedroom to look for *Dodger Daze and Knights*. I could see the packed shelves from where I stood, the books' spines creating a colorful mosaic against the wall.

I sat on the sofa and took in the living room. Hanging across from me on the wall, there was a beautifully framed and autographed photo of several Dodgers, including Carl Erskine, Clem Labine, Don Zimmer, and the Duke himself. Sitting atop an end table next to me were what looked like scorecards neatly placed inside glass frames. I took a closer look and saw that they were indeed scorecards of Dodgers games during their glorious 1955 World Series–winning season.

Norm came back from the bedroom. He held a bat in his hand, not a book. It was shiny and chestnut brown, and he twirled it around until I could read the barrel. It was a special factory-made bat with a dark oval inscription that said: "Louisville Norm Schimmel Slugger." It was signed with a Sharpie by Duke Snider.

I tried to conceal my disappointment as best I could. "Norman, that bat is awesome, but what about the book?"

He said he couldn't find it. My face became a desperate mask. Norman assured me not to worry. The book was probably down in Florida with the rest of his collection. He promised to dig it up and ship it to me.

I didn't know what to think. I was grateful to have met Schimmel, but the facts just didn't add up. Now I knew I had to get back to the office to start chasing down these three new leads that I thought would finally allow me to blow the lid off this mystery—*Dodger Daze and Knights,* Tommy Holmes, and most important of all, Helen Fawn.

Sportswriter Tommy Holmes wrote for several newspapers, including the *Brooklyn Daily Eagle,* the *New York Herald Tribune,* and the *Sporting News. Courtesy of the Sporting News/ZUMA Press*

"The Best Baseball Writer of His Time"

Wednesday, October 3, 1951

Tommy Holmes sat on a spindle-back wooden chair in the press box behind home plate, second level. His thinning hair was slicked back with Brylcreem, and he wore a white, short-sleeve dress shirt, dark slacks, and black leather shoes. He sat not far from Red Smith, who wore black-framed glasses across his oblong face. Holmes, an avowed Dodger fan, called out, "That's not how the Giants wanted to start things off today."

It was the second inning of the biggest game of the year, and the Giants' third baseman, Bobby Thomson, had just tried to occupy second base after a drive to left field. Unfortunately for Thomson, his teammate Whitey Lockman was already there. Thomson was called out. The Giants were already down, and they had just squandered a chance against Don Newcombe, who often got stronger as the game went on.

"He might have six months to think about that one," Holmes went on, perched in his usual position over a typewriter. The press box was more crowded than it had been all year. There were reporters in from all over the country to see which of these longtime rivals would advance to the World Series.

Just then the voice of William Goodrich came over the press-box PA system, "Thomson has now hit safely in fifteen consecutive games."

"That's a macabre statistic," Smith joked.

At the start of the seventh inning, Goodrich's voice could once again be heard, noting to no one in particular that Newcombe had now pitched twenty-one consecutive scoreless innings. But that streak was in serious jeopardy. Monte Irvin took a slight lead off third base, and Bobby Thomson stood at home plate. Newcombe was confident, throwing strike after strike to Thomson, four in a row. Thomson couldn't make solid contact, but he did manage to foul two of the pitches off and out of play. Newcombe geared up for his fifth pitch, and Thomson got under it. He lifted a fly ball to Snider in center field, deep enough to score Irvin from third and level the game at one run apiece. The Giants once again had hope.

But that hope was dampened very quickly. In the eighth inning, the Dodgers went back to work. Pee Wee Reese led off with a base hit to right. Duke Snider also laced a single to right, allowing Reese to advance to third base. Jackie Robinson stepped up to bat. Managers Charlie Dressen and Leo Durocher were now playing a game of cat and mouse. If Snider stole second base, Reese might try to swipe home on the throw. That run would break the 1-1 tie. So Durocher called for a pitchout, but the Duke's spikes remained planted in the dirt outside of first. Smith and Holmes and the rest of the scribes typed away as they watched the action.

The next pitch by Maglie was a curveball, but it bounced short of home plate and went past Westrum—a wild pitch. Reese darted home; 2-1 Dodgers. There is an old baseball adage that you don't root in the press box, but Holmes couldn't contain his smile. Things were once again looking good for his guys.

Then Durocher, the crafty strategist, instructed Maglie to intentionally walk Robinson to set up a possible double play. But the plan backfired. Andy Pafko hit a hard grounder to Thomson at third. Holmes's first thought was that it would be a double play, but Thomson muffed it. The ball ricocheted off his glove, scooting far enough away for Snider to score: 3-1 Dodgers.

Then Billy Cox got into the act, smashing a one-hopper right at Thomson that flashed by his ear and into the outfield, scoring Robinson.

"I think Thomson could have had both of those," Smith said to Holmes.

"Those are the perils of having an inexperienced third baseman out there for the biggest game of the year," Holmes replied.

The half inning came to its staggering end with the Dodgers ahead 4-1. Press-box typewriter keys danced up and down about how Thomson was the goat of the Giants—a base-running blunder in the second and now two plays not made in the eighth. Only his sacrifice fly in the seventh and a double in the fifth kept his day from being a total disaster.

Goodrich's voice announced that Cox would be credited with a hit, no error for Thomson.

Holmes chimed in: "That should have been an error. It sure has been an up-and-down day for Thomson."

Tommy Holmes didn't know the half of it. He was typing away, working on his article for the next day's paper. He had a unique typing style because a boyhood accident left him with only one forearm. He pecked out notes about how this was the third year in a row in which the Dodgers' season had come down to the last day. In 1949, they won the pennant in the tenth inning of their 154th game. In 1950, they lost the pennant in the tenth inning of their 154th game. Here they were heading to the ninth inning of their 157th game, and Holmes and the rest of the Dodger faithful prayed there would be no tenth inning to sweat through.

In the bottom of the eight, Newcombe continued to roll along. The Giants went down quietly, without even getting a man on base. It took Newcombe only ten pitches to dispatch them. The Dodgers were just three outs away from the National League pennant. Smith and Holmes noticed that a few wives of Giants players were being heckled in their seats by Dodger fans. They retreated to the ladies lounge beneath the stands.

"That's classless behavior by your fellow Dodger fans," Smith observed.

Holmes agreed. "I can't imagine it being good luck, either."

The top of the ninth was smooth sailing for the Giants. Durocher put Larry Jansen in to pitch and he set the hot-hitting opponents down in short order, throwing only nine pitches—eight were strikes. Between innings in the dugout, Newcombe told Dressen that although he was getting tired, he still had enough gas to polish off the Giants. But in reality, he was running on fumes. The first batter, Alvin Dark, hit a soft grounder that eluded the glove of first baseman Gil Hodges *for a leadoff single. Dressen phoned the bullpen coach Clyde Sukeforth to ask who might be ready to replace Newcombe and get the biggest outs of the year if Newcombe couldn't continue. Carl Erskine and Ralph Branca were the choices.*

The next batter, Don Mueller, hit another ground ball past Gil Hodges for a base hit. Hodges had been holding Dark on first for some reason, which allowed the ball to squeeze between Hodges and Robinson. First and second and still nobody out. Then Monte Irvin popped out to Hodges in foul territory. The Dodgers needed just two more outs. Holmes and the rest of their fans held their collective breath. Maybe Newcombe could come through and produce a double-play grounder to end it.

Whitey Lockman stepped up to home plate with one goal in mind—extend the Giants season any way he could. He pounced on Newcombe's second pitch, whizzing a streak down the left-field line for a double, scoring Dark. As Mueller raced to third, he slid awkwardly into the base, fracturing his left fibula. As he went off on a stretcher, the scoreboard read Dodgers 4, Giants 2. The Polo Grounds was buzzing.

Holmes said to Smith, "The big man has to come out. Any baseball man can see he's exhausted."

Indeed it was the end of the line for Newcombe. Dressen still had a big decision to make. He called to Sukeforth one final time for a status report on the pitchers warming up in the bullpen. As the phone rang, Erskine had just squeezed a curveball too tight, bouncing it five feet in front of the bullpen catcher. After hearing that, Dressen chose Branca to put the fire out.

Smith asked Holmes, "What do you think of bringing in Branca here?"

Holmes answered, "Thomson did just homer off Branca the other day. But the situation calls for a power pitcher, which Branca is. The other options available to Dressen aren't really strong-arm guys."

Smith asked Holmes, "Should Dressen have Branca walk Thomson? He'd be putting the winning run on base, but then he'd get to pitch to the dead-end kids at the bottom of the lineup."

"I'm glad it's not my decision. If this goes wrong, the second guessers will be out in droves."

Thomson was still standing near third base, bat in hand, watching Mueller being carried off on an old army stretcher. Durocher walked Thomson toward home plate, putting his arm around his shoulder and saying something in his ear.

Branca threw only two pitches to Thomson; the second landed out of the ballpark. Smith was astounded. In his twenty-three years of covering baseball, he'd never seen anything like it. He started typing his lead right away: "Now it is done. Now the story ends. And there is no way to tell it. The art of fiction is dead. Reality has strangled invention. Only the utterly impossible, the inexpressibly fantastic, can ever be plausible again."

He looked over to where his friend Holmes had been sitting, but Holmes was long gone. As soon as the ball landed, he scurried out of the press box. He had an idea for a story that no one else would have.

BACK AT THE office on West Twenty-seventh Street, I didn't know what to do next. I figured it couldn't hurt to send Brendan over to the New York Public Library to find a copy of *Dodger Daze and Knights*. I would have gone myself, but by this point, I thought it was a fool's errand—some of the evidence pointed to the notion that *Dodger Daze* was just a figment of Norman Schimmel's imagination.

Still, I wanted Brendan to be prepared, just in case. Before he left, I told him to bring a digital camera in case they wouldn't let him check the phantom vintage book out of the library. That way he could at least snap a few shots of the pages with pertinent information. Brendan cleared security in the lobby of the library and was directed to room 315, the Bill Blass Public Catalog Room. If anybody was going to find our book, it would be Brendan, who had spent the last four years doing library research.

He passed through the Bill Blass section of the catalog room—a subsection of the Rose Main Reading Room. It's in the Rose room that the catalog search actually takes place. His greatest chance of finding the book was there. The room is beautiful. Forty-two white oak wood tables in perfectly aligned rows are surrounded by seventeen-foot-tall bronze arched windows. The original chandelier fixtures overflowing with hundreds of lightbulbs illuminate the pristine wooden bookcases, chairs, brass railings, and a plaster ceiling that's decorated with ornate paintings trimmed with gold and copper designs.

He spoke to a librarian named Gloria, who had worked in the library as a volunteer for more than forty years. She had nearly white hair and wore a pair of large, pink-framed eyeglasses dangling from a metal chain around her neck. He asked her if she could help him acquire a copy of *Dodger Daze and Knights*. "I'm not even sure this book exists," he told Gloria.

Gloria told him, "If your book was ever published, it's somewhere in this library. Bet your bottom dollar on it." The people down in the central archives section in the trenches of the library searched for the old title as he anxiously waited upstairs.

Brendan waited, not really sure what to expect at this point. Ten minutes later, a pile of books was hoisted up on the old dumbwaiter that the library uses to transport books from the stacks underneath Bryant Park to the various floors throughout the building. Gloria grabbed a long, narrow, black hardcover from the pile of books.

"I guess your book exists after all," she said as she handed him a copy of *Dodger Daze and Knights*. The catalog data on the spine read: "Holmes MVFB 1953." Brendan pulled up a seat at a table and switched on the bronze table lamp. He cracked the worn spine and the pages smelled old and musty, the scent of a book that hadn't been opened in decades.

He started with the table of contents. Before long, he had something fascinating, if not exactly what we were looking for. He pulled his Canon PowerShot out of his backpack and snapped a few pictures from the book. Brendan sprinted back to Twenty-seventh Street with new and vital information in his backpack.

I was in the edit room when he arrived. He had a giant grin on his face, like a man who had just won the lottery. He pulled out his digital camera and showed me the pictures he had snapped. There it was in black and white. Buried deep in chapter 22 of *Dodger Daze and Knights,* Tommy Holmes casually mentions that the Thomson home-run ball landed in the lap of a woman named Helen Gawn, with a G.

"Schimmel had it almost exactly right!" Brendan exulted.

I was so excited, I was nearly shouting. "Not too bad for a guy remembering something from fifty years ago! He was only *one* letter off!"

And this certainly explained why I'd had no luck finding Helen Fawn. I did a quick Google search for Helen Gawn, but it was no more productive. But at least now I knew I was looking for the right person. I was going to have to lean on my police and law contacts to find out who she was.

First I had another mission, though. The exact wording of Holmes's passage about the fate of the ball bothered me a little bit: "Ralph Branca threw a fastball where Bobby Thomson was swinging his bat and a three-run homer landed in the lap of a lady in the left-field stands. The lady's name is unofficially reported to be Helen Gawn."

What exactly did he mean by "unofficially reported"? Was Holmes just reporting what someone else had told him? If so, how reliable could the information be? Probably not very, but it was crucial that I prove how Tommy Holmes could have known who caught the ball.

I tried to contact the *Brooklyn Eagle* to see if Holmes's game notes might be archived somewhere. That idea was dead in the water when I learned that the daily version of the *Eagle* folded its tents the same year the Brooklyn Dodgers won their last World Series—1955.

Brendan and I divided up some research responsibilities. He searched the library archives to try to identify the reporters who were in the locker rooms after the game. He found winners' locker-room quotes from Ed Sinclair of the *New York Herald Tribune,* John Drebinger and James Dawson of the *New York Times,* Milton Richman of United Press, and Jim McCulley of the *Daily News.* Over in the losers' locker room, huddled around the sullen, wordless figure of Ralph Branca, were Les Biederman of the *Pittsburgh Press,* Will Grimsley of Associated Press, and Roscoe McGowen of the *New York Times.*

I found this encouraging, but it wasn't enough. Just because Tommy Holmes *wasn't* in the clubhouse didn't mean that he *was* in the stands. Finally, I was able to find Tommy Holmes's actual game account from the *Brooklyn Eagle* on microfilm. The line about Helen Gawn from *Dodger Daze and Knights* appeared almost verbatim, and he didn't use any quotes from the locker room, suggesting that he may have gone into the stands himself and wasn't merely relying on hearsay.

Later that same day, I finally heard back from the Hall of Fame. They supplied me with enough information to paint a helpful portrait of the man currently at the center of the mystery. Tommy Holmes was born in 1904. He lived and worked his entire life in New York. He lost his left forearm as a young boy in an unspecified accident. He overcame the handicap to become one of the greatest sportswriters of his time with both the *Brooklyn Daily Eagle* newspaper and the *New York Herald Tribune.* He was so interested in baseball that covering the Dodgers every day for one paper wasn't enough. He was also the Brooklyn Dodgers correspondent for the *Sporting News.*

He served as the national president of the Baseball Writers Association of America in 1947 and was well liked by his peers. His writing style was old school before there was an old school. Red Smith—a God of sports reporters—described his work as "reactionary yet unpretentious." He died of a heart attack at the State University Hospital of Downstate Medical Center in Brooklyn on March 27, 1975.

Brendan and I reconvened in the edit room for a brainstorming session. I picked up the faxed pages from the Hall of Fame, which included various articles written by Red Smith. Smith referred to Holmes as "the best baseball writer of his time, possibly the best of all time."

Brendan took the fax from me and leafed through it. While he read through it, I began thinking out loud.

"We know Holmes had a handicap. Smith specifically mentions how it affected him his entire life—he always wanted to do more than anyone else, to prove himself to be the best."

Brendan found the exact quote from Smith and read it to me, "Tommy had always said the injury gave him an inferiority complex. He was a long time overcoming it."

He put the paper down, and our eyes met. We were thinking the exact same thing. "I see where you're going with this," Brendan said while nodding his head.

"Think about it," I said. Holmes felt like he had to prove himself every day. He was a Dodger fan at heart, he had just had his heart broken, but instead of sitting there moping, he knew he had to do his job."

Brendan picked up my line of thought. "He didn't want to just do his job. He wanted to do it better than everybody else because that's the way he always did things."

I took it a step further, "Maybe finding the person who caught the ball was some kind of personal mission."

Then Brendan asked me the key question. "How would Holmes have gotten from the press box out to section 35 so quickly?"

I ran over the blueprint of the Polo Grounds in my head. I knew the layout pretty well after months looking at stadium photos, watching game footage, and talking to fans like Schimmel.

The press box was in the typical place, second level behind home plate, maybe a little skewed toward third base. But the reporters had easy access down to field level. That's how they mobbed Thomson so fast as he crossed home plate. I shared this information with the group.

"That makes sense," Brendan said. "But how would Holmes get into the left-field stands to interview the person who caught the ball?"

"There's that stairway that led up into the clubhouse in left center field, beneath the Chesterfield sign."

I pulled up two photographs of the stairway Eddie Logan had talked about, which were stored on the hard drive that held the film. Brendan was bowled over.

"It's really not so complicated. To get there, all he'd have to do is run across the field to that staircase, and he'd be into those seats. It's about a hundred yards away but he had half his arm missing, not half his leg."

"So you're saying that as the celebration was going on, as everyone was running toward Thomson at home plate—"

I was so excited now that I cut him off. "Holmes would be running in the opposite direction—toward the outfield!"

As I looked more closely at the documents the Hall of Fame sent over, I became even more convinced that we were correct. Back in the old days of newspapers, there were both morning and afternoon papers—and sometimes different versions of each paper. The morning papers were typically filled with news of what had happened the previous day. The afternoon papers had plenty of that as well, but were a little more geared toward feature stories—articles that would go a little deeper, so people would want to read them when they already knew the basic facts of the story. Holmes wrote for an afternoon paper. In an interview with *Editor and Publisher,* Holmes said that even though the morning man might write two to three times more than his afternoon colleague, it's still "more difficult to do a consistently good job" when reporting for an afternoon paper. "You're always looking for a second-day angle," he added, "and more often than not, there is no obvious angle."

A second-day angle that was not obvious? That sounded to me like a story about the person who caught the ball that was so meaningful, it was immediately dubbed the "Shot Heard 'Round the World."

Another article about Holmes mentioned that he was more of a sports historian than a hobbyist. He had a massive library of the baseball and boxing cards put out by Sweet Caporal cigarettes, predecessors of today's bubblegum cards. As "reactionary" as his writing might have been, Holmes was also ahead of his time! Back in a day when no one was interested in memorabilia, Holmes was already collecting it. Maybe that same interest led him to wonder about the fate of the baseball.

I still needed to prove that Holmes went out to left field himself. Several minutes of newsreel footage from the game had been sent over by Major League Baseball. It included the whole postgame celebration, complete with fans running on the field, the players picking Thomson up on their shoulders, and all the general mayhem on the Polo Grounds infield. I had watched the footage before but hadn't spotted anything out of the ordinary.

Brendan scrambled to find the tape from Major League Baseball. We watched it on the big monitor.

Inching closer to the monitor, Brendan was getting all revved up. "So if we're right about this, we should be able to see a reporter in the midst of the celebration, heading straight out to section 35."

I played the footage, watching frame by frame. I could hardly believe what I saw. Sure enough, as bedlam ensued on the field, and everyone else ran toward Thomson at home plate, there was one man in a white short-sleeve shirt, dark dress slacks, and black shoes darting across the field, heading toward the left-field stands. Looking closely, we had our proof. The man had only one forearm.

It was Tommy Holmes.

TWELVE

Eyewitness

Wednesday, October 3, 1951

Irving Aks was a legend on the streets and in the candy stores throughout Brooklyn back in the fifties. A passionate Dodgers fan known to one and all by his initials, I.A., he would do or say pretty much anything to support his boys in blue. Rarely would a day go by that I.A. wasn't holding court on his stoop at 488 New Jersey Avenue in the East New York section of Brooklyn.

Irv was what you might call a nice Jewish boy. Even into young adulthood, he lived with his parents to help make their lives easier. He worked part-time at his big brother Ruby's neighborhood flower shop—when the job didn't interfere with attending or listening to a Dodgers game. When it came to Dem Bums, as the team was affectionately known throughout the borough, I.A. had a passion unrivaled by even the nuttiest of fans. Irv didn't have much money, but he couldn't resist the temptation to watch the Dodgers at Ebbets Field, so he often climbed the fences, sneaking in for free to see Brooklyn play.

In early October 1951, Ruby decided to give his little brother a surprise gift to commemorate what he hoped would be a World Series appearance for the Dodgers. Ruby had spent two days building a special funeral wreath out of red and white carnations and various foliage, mounted on a freestanding easel. In the center of the circular wreath was a black ribbon with large white script letters that spelled out the words "Sympathy to the Giants." The day before the deciding game, Ruby told Irv to take the funeral wreath to the Polo Grounds. After the Dodgers won, he was to run onto the field and stick the wreath in the dirt near home plate—an exclamation mark for the Dodgers' glorious victory.

There was just one problem: Irv did not have a ticket. Ruby challenged his younger brother to figure something out. After all, he was notorious for sneaking into dozens of Dodger games at Ebbets. Why couldn't he sneak into a game at the Polo Grounds? Irv accepted the challenge. He took a five-cent subway ride up to the Polo Grounds the night before, climbed up a water pipe, and snuck into the stadium just after midnight. He hoisted the wreath up into the stadium with twenty-pound-test fishing line. But he was not the only one at the ballpark that night. Several fans were sleeping on the sidewalk, waiting for the ticket booth to open the next morning. This attracted the police, and one of the cops spotted Irv climbing up onto the first tier of the stadium, and he ordered him to come down, threatening to ticket him for trespassing. But Irv was as stubborn as he was devoted to his Dodgers. He refused to climb down, and the police were not willing to risk their necks by climbing up. Before Irv disappeared into the night, a few photographers—on hand to shoot the story of zealous fans sleeping out for tickets—snapped shots of I.A. holding the funeral wreath. Armed with Ruby's wreath and a cheese sandwich, Irv found an open janitor's closet to hide in and catch a little sleep. The next afternoon, he found a vacant seat in the outfield section, just to the right of the left-field foul pole.

Thomson's home run was in Irving's line of vision the whole time. As the ball was in flight, he yelled aloud, "Curve, curve foul!" It never curved. When the ball sailed over Andy Pafko's head, Irv dropped the funeral wreath in disgust. He just sat there reflecting on another lost season.

THANKS TO NORMAN Schimmel, I now knew all about Tommy Holmes and how he ran to the stands to hunt for the fate of the ball. Piece by piece, I felt like the mystery was coming together. I was energized but still didn't have everything I would need. I really wanted to know what happened once Holmes made it out to section 35. Did he actually speak to Helen Gawn? Or was she just pointed out to him by someone sitting nearby?

I could hardly sleep at night. A small part of me was scared that once the hunt came to an end, I'd have nothing important to do with my life. I knew, from the therapy I'd done when I was severely depressed, that one thing that helped bring me out of it was pursuing a goal. When I focused my energy in the right place, there was hardly anything I couldn't accomplish. At least that's how I felt. But now I had no idea what would come next.

I was also concerned about telling my dad the latest news about the ball, figuring that he'd probably be defensive, as he was when Thomson claimed that the Giants had never signed the ball. But now that I had tangible evidence linking the ball to this woman, it seemed even more unlikely to me that his ball was the Thomson ball. It was probably just a cool relic with some sweet autographs and a Ford Frick stamp that was probably worth some money but not near what he was hoping for. After all he'd done for me, I hated to disappoint him. Regardless, I knew that the most important thing was learning the truth.

Like most kids, I had always sought my dad's approval. And if I could find out the truth about the ball, I hoped I'd be a star in the eyes of my hero—my dad. He chose me for this mission, and I wasn't going to let him down or hide anything I found from him. Still, I didn't feel the need to give him a possibly disappointing update until I had a little more information.

I knew I had a couple of choices for my next move. I could launch a full-fledged hunt for anyone in America named Helen Gawn. I already knew that this would take a lot more than a quick Internet search. I would have to start from the bottom up, going back to my journalist and police contacts. But before I took this leap, I brought my mom back into the loop, asking her not to tell Dad what I was up to yet. I was certain she could point me in the right direction, and I knew she enjoyed helping me out. I was a little worried about leaning on her so much, because she had some health issues. She'd had a full hip replacement years earlier and lived in a lot of pain but never complained about it. Driving was becoming more and more difficult for her, so whenever possible, I volunteered to take her to the one place I knew she looked forward to going to all week—the beauty parlor. Tudor Village Beauty Salon was located on Pitkin Avenue in Ozone Park, Queens, one town north of my folks' house in Howard Beach, where I was still staying.

Mom and I loved listening to WFAN sports talk-show host Steve Somers during the short car drive. She got a kick out of his New York–centric way of speaking, even though he's originally from San Francisco. He'd often use Yiddish expressions that Mom and I were both familiar with, and we would laugh out loud.

"What, already with these Mets? They're enough to make you meshugana," Somers would bark out after a particularly bad loss. Mom always said she liked him so much because his patter re-minded her of the way her own father spoke. One Saturday, we drove to Tudor Village and Somers was doing his full-blown shtick. "Next up on the line is Bruce from Bayside. Hello, Bruce-a-la." Turning the volume down, I told Mom how I was trying to find an eyewitness from the game, but it felt like I was looking for the pro-verbial needle in a haystack.

"What have you done so far?"

"I tried contacting some of the players from both the Giants and Dodgers, but it's nearly impossible," I grumbled. "Either they're no longer around, they don't return my calls, or they have absolutely no recollection of what happened at one game fifty-five years ago."

Then, as in the past, she put her sensational problem-solving skills into motion.

"What about a fan? Someone at the game who is still alive. Have you looked for any of those?"

I had considered putting out a call to anyone who was at the game, but I was convinced it would be in vain. Why would they be paying attention to what was happening in the stands when there was all that pandemonium to take in on the field? After I explained this to Mom, she said something that led to a breakthrough.

She pointed out that I needed to find a fan who was sitting in or near section 35 so that their attention would be on the ball, not on Thomson.

Suddenly it hit me: Listening to Somers talking with his Yiddish expressions helped me remember that I already knew just such a man.

After the first flurry of phone calls, I had told my mom about Irving, the guy who called in about the Lockman double and sounded just like my grandfather.

"*Irving was at the game!*" I reminded her. "I think he was sitting in the outfield. Maybe he wasn't far from where the ball landed. He could have seen Holmes!"

I drove into Manhattan late that same Saturday night itching to listen to Irving's message again. The building was closed, but I had a key. The hallways were dark up on the twelfth floor, but I had brought a little flashlight that I kept in a survival kit in the trunk of my car. I made my way to the front door of Heavy Light and twisted the key in the doorknob. Inside the edit room, I fired up the machine, and the start-up *pong* noise reverberated off the walls because it was so quiet in there. I was alone in the dark edit room and the place took on a spooky feel, but I felt the presence of my mom, who'd been such a help to me.

I sifted through the electronic lists of phone messages and found Irving's.

"I'm calling about the article I read in the newspaper about the Shot Heard 'Round the World. I didn't catch the ball, but I was at the game. I sat in foul territory in the left-field stands near the pole. . . ." I wrote down Irving's phone number, as I was pretty sure the location he described was in section 33 or 34, just one or two sections away from where the home run landed.

There weren't any other relevant details in the message, but I thought if I sat down with Irving, I could jog his memory. There were no guarantees.

So as I had done with Schimmel, I had Brendan arrange to film my discussion with Irving for the documentary. By Thursday of that week, we had a day scheduled for the crew to drive out to meet Irv in Flushing, Queens. We arrived at Irving's two-floor apartment building off Main Street and Seventy-first Avenue around lunchtime.

His wife laid out an impressive spread of food for us: turkey, bologna, cheese, onion buns, cream cheese, and coleslaw. None of us knew her real name because he kept calling her Red or Red Jobs, (expressions from the fifties designating women who dyed their hair red).

Irv was seventy-seven years old, had a gorgeous head of brown and gray hair, unusually large ears, and a belly that suggested he frequently ate well. Dressed in a dark green velour long-sleeve shirt and worn-out jeans, he merrily greeted us at the door like a kind-hearted grandfather. Before we could set our coats down, Irv was trying to get us to eat.

"Are you fellas hungry?

"Thanks, but maybe we'll grab a bite a little bit later," I replied.

Pointing toward his wife, he leaned in and whispered to us, "She didn't cook any of it, so don't worry. I ordered in sandwiches from the deli. If you like, just have a nosh—maybe a schmear on a soft onion bun. What do you say?"

We assured Irving that we'd take him up on his generous offer later on, then settled into the living room. He took me through the story of how he snuck into the Polo Grounds the night before the game with the funeral wreath. Red Jobs stood in the background, silently looking on. Her expressionless face told me she had probably heard this story more times than she could count.

"After I was up there, the cops told me to come down. I just ignored them."

Waving his hand, he spoke in a comic voice in the same manner as he did to the authorities that night: "Hel-lo, *of-fi-cer.*"

The game started at 1:20 P.M., so I asked Irv how he didn't get noticed by a security guard or grounds-crew member after the stadium opened in the morning. He let out a grin from one outsized ear to the other, and it was obvious that he was as proud as a peacock.

"Listen to this one, yeah? I found an old broom and a maintenance man's cap in the custodial room that I slept in. And the morning of the game, I posed as a Polo Grounds employee!"

I laughed out loud as Irv relived the moment, imitating how he spoke to the *real* employees—true Giants fans—while pushing his broom through the bleachers.

"Good morning! We're going to send them back to Brooklyn today, huh, fella."

"Dem Bums really are just that . . . a bunch of bums."

"Great day for a pennant win, eh?"

"It was the hardest thing I ever did in my life, pretending to be a Giants fan, even for an hour."

Irving noted that the *New York Times* called him "eccentric" in their account of his stealth mission that night.

"What do you mean?" I asked while stifling a laugh.

"Well, I had my picture in all the newspapers the next day, holding the wreath." Irv slid his rounded body to the edge of the couch. "Wait, I'll show you."

He walked off into his bedroom. Red Jobs slipped into the den. After a few moments, Irv reappeared in the living room holding a gigantic envelope. Sure enough, a picture of Irving made the front page of the next day's papers (the *Brooklyn Daily Eagle*, *New York World Telegram and Sun,* and even the *New York Times*). Inside the envelope were copies of the yellow-colored newspapers with Irving's picture. He wanted to set them down on the table where the sandwiches were.

"You fellas want to help me out? Let's clear the decks and make some room here."

Brendan and the rest of the film crew carried the food and drinks into the kitchen, while I chatted up Irv and looked through his newspaper stash. One by one, Irv pulled out the articles, which he had mounted on thick brown cardboard. As real as life, there he was. Every paper had the same photo of Irving holding the wreath with his name in the caption.

Before I asked Irv about Tommy Holmes, I wanted demonstrable proof that he definitely had sat near section 35. In his phone message, he'd said he was in the left-field stands near the foul pole. Seeing Irving's picture in the newspaper reminded me that the wide angle of the flea-market picture actually *showed* the foul pole. Luckily I had both images (*Pafko at the Wall* and the flea-market shot) scanned onto my laptop, which was in my bag.

"Irv, you think you could spot yourself in a photo from the game?"

"How's that possible?"

"Oh, you'd be surprised what's possible these days," I replied with self-assurance.

I pulled out my laptop and opened the images folder. Accidentally, I clicked on *Pafko at the Wall*. Irv reacted immediately.

"There's Andy Pafko! Big number forty-eight. Oh, this brings back memories." Seeing the image of that heartbreaking moment made him emotional, just like Sal Marchiano.

"I'll tell you this. It was a good shot—a line shot," he said. Then his voice trailed back down. "I'll never forget watching that ball sail over poor Pafko's head. Oy vey."

I minimized the picture on my screen and opened the flea-market photo.

"Look at that picture. God! That's unbelievable," Irv gushed.

As I increased the size of the photo on my screen I asked Irv if he could remember exactly where he sat.

"Well, let me see. There's the foul pole, so I should be just a little towards the left." He pointed out the general area.

Using the foul pole as a guide, I worked my eyes up and down, back and forth in the vicinity Irving indicated.

"It's so difficult to see. Can't you make it any bigger?"

I zoomed in closer on the photo to 125 percent, then 150, now 175. We both looked for a face that resembled Irv. Brendan leaned in to look as well. Then I saw it. While using the grid search technique Hal Sherman taught me, I spotted a face buried among the masses who looked familiar. And it was right where Irving said he sat. The man in the photo had the same fabulous hairline that Irving's managed to keep all these years. I pointed my finger.

"I think that's you, Irv."

"You got to be kidding me."

"I'm not kidding. That looks just like you. Look at the hair, the nose . . ."

Dodgers fan Irving Aks snuck into the Polo Grounds the night before
the game and sat in the left-field stands. *From the author's collection*

He leaned in to the computer screen, squinting his eyes, looking
directly at the face in the crowd. He asked me to make it bigger
still. I zoomed in to 250 percent. The image was getting pixilated,
but was still surprisingly clear. Irv shook his head in disbelief.

"That could be me. You got to be kidding me. That could be me!"

First the detectives find the ball in the first photo, and now I'm
on the verge of spotting my eyewitness in a second vintage photo. I
was getting good at this. I continued enhancing the picture on my
computer screen for Irving. He was nearly convinced and called to
his wife in the other room.

"Red Jobs! Come here! I need you to confirm something. It's like
an FBI thing going on out here. It's unbelievable."

Red joined us huddled around the computer.

"I think they found me in the photo," Irv said.

She looked on, nonplussed.

Irving pointed toward the computer screen, but didn't reveal which man we thought he was. "This is the foul pole. I was sitting just to the left of it."

Leaning in, she studied the people sitting near the foul pole. Then, with complete certainty she revealed her finding—it was the same man we'd been looking at.

"There! That's you. The hair, the nose, the ear."

"You found me? Are you sure?"

"No one else has an ear like that." Red had given me the proof I was looking for.

I asked Irv to tell me exactly what he remembered happening after the game.

"I dropped the wreath and just sat in my seat. I didn't want to move."

"What about other people. Did they stick around or just leave, or what?

Taking a sip from his Diet Coke, he casually mentioned, "I suppose it depended on what team you rooted for. I was probably one of the only Dodger fans who stayed. I didn't want to be seen with the wreath. I probably would have taken a beating."

Irv explained that he had sat in his seat until the entire section was nearly empty. He figured a reporter might want to interview him about the wreath, but since the Dodgers lost, he didn't want any part of it. "They knew I had the wreath, because my picture was in the morning paper. But they didn't know where I was sitting. Then I saw this one reporter come up into the stands. I didn't want him to find me, so I dropped the wreath, crouched in my chair, and kept an eye on him."

I couldn't believe what I was hearing. Irv remembered seeing a reporter go out to section 35.

Irving continued. "I saw him talking to some fans—I was close enough to see all that."

"Irv, do you remember which reporter it was?"

"No, I wouldn't know one from the other, but he was up in section 35."

I asked if he had any idea why a reporter was up in the stands, when there was all that celebrating going on around home plate?

Irv thought for a second, "I suppose he was looking, or asking, 'Did anyone get the ball?'"

There was just one piece of the information missing now. "Did you see him talking to anyone in particular?"

"He talked to a bunch of people. I remember him talking to this one woman. He followed her out as she was trying to leave. I was just relieved he was going in the opposite direction from me."

The time had arrived. It was Helen Gawn or bust.

Private Detectives

It seemed obvious to me that Helen Gawn either wasn't alive or didn't want to be found. Otherwise, she surely would have stepped forward at some point, saying she had the ball, especially with the surge in interest in the memorabilia market in the five decades since the Thomson game. I figured it would take a true professional crime solver to find the mystery lady from left field. The first person I approached was Detective Sherman, who had helped me spot the ball in the photo using his blood spatter technique, eye-line theory, and grid search. Detective Sherman was willing to help but told me that finding people just wasn't his area of expertise. Detective Austin told me much the same thing.

As I weighed my options, it became abundantly clear who could help me—my photojournalist friend, Susan Watts. She had introduced me to Sherman and Austin in the first place, and I figured she might know someone I could call right away. Susan is a real networker, the kind of person who seemingly knows everybody. Her photo assignments down at City Hall over the years gave her connections not just with police and politicians, but also many of

their affiliates, including attorneys, fund-raisers, and—most important for me now—private detectives.

My hunch was correct, as Susan almost immediately gave me the
names of two private detectives who worked together. Here, I'll
call them Joey and Greg. They told me up front that they didn't
want their real names mentioned or their faces shown anywhere
in the film. As Joey told me during our first phone call, "Then we
wouldn't be *private* detectives anymore, would we, Brian?"

I decided to tap the film's budget for their retainer—a difficult
financial move but a necessary one. My partners on the film agreed.
After all, If we didn't find Helen Gawn, we wouldn't have a film. I
secured the retainer and arranged a meeting with Joey at an upscale
midtown Italian restaurant on a late Thursday afternoon.

He was very clear in his instructions, and they scared me a little
bit. "Come alone," he said on the phone. "No cameras, no voice re-
corders, just you, me, and my partner. Don't even tell anyone else
about the meeting." His voice was stern and forceful.

I got off the phone with him and called Susan to ask her what
his story was. She clued me in as to how private detectives operate.
She told me he had to be extremely cautious about first-time meet-
ings. Apparently, there are a lot of alimony-paying ex-husbands out
there who have serious gripes with the private detectives who caught
them in various compromising positions.

Susan assured me that Joey and Greg were two of the best in
New York at what they do, describing them as no-nonsense ex-cops
who didn't mess around. After meeting them for all of ten seconds,
I knew exactly what she meant. She didn't know much about their
background except that they retired early from the force and went
into a higher-paying area of law enforcement. They answered to
another man, who brought high-priced clients to them through his

law firm. Susan told me they'd get results. For me, those were the magic words: Results were all I cared about.

As I approached the restaurant on East Forty-sixth Street, I realized I was down the block from the infamous spot where John Gotti had sat in a parked car watching his mob soldiers gun down Gambino crime boss Paul Castellano in 1985, taking charge of the Mafia family until his own death in 2002. I started to feel a little on edge. I was supposed to be on a feel-good hunt for a baseball, and the road had led me to a secret meeting with two shady ex-cops in a notoriously mobbed-up section of Manhattan.

I had an uncomfortable feeling, entering the empty restaurant. Sinatra crooned "Fly Me to the Moon" softly in the background, and I felt like an extra in a Martin Scorsese movie. I briefly concocted the crazy theory that maybe this meeting might be some sort of set up by some Mafia don who wanted to find the ball for himself. Sure, that was just my imagination running amok, but considering all that had happened to me in the last four months, nothing seemed impossible.

Inside there was plush maroon carpet, which led to a shiny parquet floor where the bar was. The bartender sized me up as soon as I walked into the room. He said, "You're here to see Joey, right? They're in the back. Last table by the wall. Go ahead, they're expecting you."

I nodded in appreciation and started to walk toward the back. But before I even got there, two men approached me. One was somewhere between chubby and muscular with a perfectly groomed brown mustache and slicked-back brown hair. He wore a dressy black suit and black mock turtleneck. This was Joey. He had a confident yet calming air about him—as though he knew something no one else did. Behind him was Greg, a tall, fit, ruddy-faced man in a sport coat and jeans. Greg was the strong, silent type. He was clearly taking everything in.

When Joey reached his hand out to shake mine, his arm swiped across the bottom of his suit jacket, revealing a 9mm Glock in a lightweight holster strapped to his belt. I got the feeling this gesture was intentional. This was not someone I wanted to cross.

"Brian, good to meet you. This is my partner, Greg. You want a drink or something?"

I politely passed on the drink as we found seats at the bar.

Joey told me he was unclear as to exactly what I wanted because I was so vague on the phone about the woman I wanted him to find. He asked if she was my wife or some psycho stalker.

I smirked while assuring him it was nothing of the sort.

I got the impression Greg and Joey weren't used to seeing new clients smile. They both looked at me quizzically, waiting for more.

"Look, Joey. I heard you guys are really good at what you do, but this is a delicate confidential situation."

Greg and Joey exchanged glances. "Everything we take on is confidential," Joey said.

I leaned in closer and told them the whole story about my search for the Thomson ball: my dad, Thomson and Logan, Schimmel, Tommy Holmes, and how they all had led me to a mystery woman named Helen Gawn.

"I don't even know if she's dead or alive. The only thing I have is her name in black and white, Helen Gawn, G-A-W-N."

Joey and Greg looked interested. I explained once again how important it was that this information not be leaked to anyone at all, lest it find its way into the press and become front-page news. As much as I needed the media's help previously, now I needed to keep them at arm's length. If they were to find Helen Gawn before I did, the story would get out, and my film would be ruined.

While I spoke, Greg jotted down notes in a reporter's pad. I asked Joey if he thought they might be able to help. His face widened to a confident grin.

"We do stuff like this all the time. Granted, our usual work doesn't involve the Shot Heard 'Round the World, but in terms of finding people who don't want to be found, we've got decades of experience."

Greg chimed in. "We've got access to databases that could find a person on the bottom of the ocean. Don't worry. If this woman ever set foot in this country over the last two hundred years, we'll find her. Dead or alive."

Greg continued: "And on a personal level, after hearing that story you just told us, I can't wait to get started on this." His tone lightened. "Hey, if we find the ball, do we get some of the money? I bet it's worth a few mil."

Joey chimed in, "Take it easy, Cowboy. Let's find the lady first, before you go buying a Maserati."

Whatever doubts I had before meeting the private detectives, I at least knew they were committed to my cause. As Sinatra continued singing in the background, Greg started up a little baseball chatter. Just like practically everyone I had met on my hunt for the ball, he had some firsthand experience with the Thomson home run.

"My father always talked about that game. He was a big-time Dodgers fan back in the day, and he hated the Giants with a passion. That home run burned his shorts for years."

Joey couldn't resist getting into the act. "My old man was a Yankee fan, just like me. Nothing but winners in *this* family," he boasted.

They said that they'd check back in with me in about a week with their initial findings. There really was nothing I could do but wait. But my wait didn't last long. Just two days later, I got a call from Joey. He told me they were on to something. Through an unidentified source, Greg was able to check the Social Security records, and there was an exact match! He found a woman named Helen Gawn who was an adult in the 1950s. The only other thing they knew for now was that this Helen Gawn passed away in 2000.

Now that the two private detectives were hot on Helen's trail, I couldn't hold off telling my dad what was happening any longer. I was afraid to tell him the news about Helen Gawn, but I owed it to him to come clean—especially now, as I might be so close to discovering the truth. The next morning, I offered to take him for breakfast at the Water View diner on Cross Bay Boulevard near the house.

As far as he knew, I was still mainly trying to prove that his baseball could be the ball spotted in *Pafko at the Wall.* But his radar went up as soon as I muttered: "Dad, I need to tell you something about the baseball."

He looked like an employee who knew he was about to be fired. I told him about everything that had happened since the media blitz, including the most recent news. "Poppa, I have two top-notch private detectives working on this, and they just found out there was a Helen Gawn who was alive in the fifties."

Dad got upset. "What the hell does that even mean?"

Before I could even open my mouth, he cut me off.

"These private detectives you hired, did they talk to this Helen what's-her-name?" he barked.

"No, Da. She died in 2000."

He took a giant sip of coffee. "Where was she from? Brooklyn? Manhattan? Can they prove she was at the game?"

"Dad, it's really complicated," I said earnestly. "All the information isn't back yet."

"Fine. I understand that. Let me just ask you one question then. Is there any way these private detectives could trace her back to the Salvation Army?"

"I'm not sure I'm following you."

"How do you know that she didn't donate the ball to the thrift shop? If they're so good at their job, they should be able to come up with some paperwork that could place her in the Levittown thrift shop in 1990. You ever think of that?"

I couldn't disagree with him. I had mostly given up on the idea that Dad's ball was the Thomson ball when Thomson himself told me that the ball was never signed and after I read what Tommy Holmes wrote about Helen Gawn. But the more I thought about it, I couldn't deny the possibility that maybe Helen was able to somehow arrange to have the ball signed by the team without ever telling them which ball it was. If it turned out that Helen Gawn lived on Long Island at the end of her life—a distinct possibility, it now seemed to me—I would be just one step away from proving that Dad's ball was indeed the miracle ball.

A week passed and there was no word from Joey. I left several anxious messages on his voice mail until he finally got back to me. He spoke in a guarded and unemotional tone with none of the exuberance of our last conversation. I wasn't sure if that meant good news or bad news.

Unfortunately, it was the latter. Joey laid out the facts for me. At the time of her death, Helen shared a post office box in Atascadero, California, with one Martha M. Verheyen. Joey tracked down Ms. Verheyen, who told him that Helen was her grandmother and confirmed that she passed away in 2000. But she was definitely not our Helen Gawn, because in 1951, her name was Helen Chambers. She only became Helen Gawn after she married in the mid-1960s. Ms. Verheyen added that her grandmother had never even been to New York. This lead was dead. Dropping my head, I continued to listen in silence.

"Brian, you still there?"

"I'm here, Joey."

"I have a little more bad news. There aren't any other Helen Gawns who could have been there that day. Starting in 1920, twenty-six people died in this country with the surname Gawn. But none had the first or middle name Helen."

I was getting desperate, but Joey still wasn't ready to give up.

"When we first met, you told me that the only thing you were sure of was that the woman's name was Helen Gawn, G-A-W-N. But now that we know there was no such person, I have to ask you, how can you be so sure of her name?"

I reminded him about Holmes's column and book.

"What exactly did Holmes write?"

I found a photocopy of the page from *Dodger Daze* and read it aloud. ". . . the woman's name is unofficially reported to be Helen Gawn."

"Unofficially reported, huh?"

I could tell his wheels were turning, and I was starting to catch his drift. After a few seconds, he continued. "Maybe Holmes reported it 'unofficially' because he didn't know how to spell it?"

I slapped the table in front of me. That phrase, "unofficially reported to be," had always bothered me, and I never did figure out what Holmes meant by it. I felt a glimmer of hope. "Joey, it sounds to me like you've got some more digging to do."

But the second search was none too successful, either. Joey and

Greg discovered that 127 people with the last name Gawne entered America through Ellis Island between 1894 and 1920. Of those, only two were named Helen. One died in California during the 1930s; the other in Illinois a decade later. They found other spellings, including Gaughn and Gaunn, but there were still no possible matches. The private detectives had struck out.

Over the next few weeks, I didn't know what to do. My search had hit a brick wall, and my movie was in serious jeopardy. After more than a year of living a normal life again, I began drifting in the wrong direction emotionally. I was feeling guilty about not being able to help my dad and feeling like a failure for not uncovering the whereabouts of Helen or the baseball. I worried that I might sink back down into a depression and didn't know if I'd be able to pull myself out again.

Sensing how down I was, Dad drove us out to Shea in late August to take in a night game. What better way to lift my spirits than to see David Wright hit one out to the opposite field or watch Jose Reyes slide headfirst into third to complete an electrifying triple?

We bought scalped tickets and had great seats. It was a muggy summer night, and it should have been great. But being at the ballpark backfired on me. Instead of enjoying the game, I just kept thinking about 1951. Shea might as well have been the Polo Grounds. Thomson and Branca, Tommy Holmes, and Helen Gawn. I was so close to putting it all together, but I had nothing to show for it, and it was eating away at me. I hadn't had a panic attack in nearly a year, but I felt one coming on. I told my dad, and he knew exactly what to do. We were up and out of there immediately.

While driving quickly home, Dad kept assuring me that everything would be all right. "Just keep breathing," he told me. "Don't worry about any of it. You've come this far, and me and Mommy are more proud of you than you'll ever know." My breath slowly began returning and I was barely able to fight down the panic attack.

As soon as I composed myself, I told my dad how much of a failure I felt like.

"A failure?" he said. "You are anything but a failure. That's ridiculous."

But it wasn't ridiculous to me. If I gave up on finding the ball, I'd feel that I'd gotten near the top of Mount Everest and then decided to crawl back down. I couldn't give up, but I had no new ideas and hardly any money left, either. I was caught in a serious rut. I tried to explain. "But I can't finish this film, and I can't think about anything else until I do."

"You have to keep working, Brian. It's what got you out of that depression in the first place. With those cops locating the ball in the photo and all that media coverage, you could still make a great film. Then that will lead to something new."

I heard what he was saying, but I felt sick inside. "It's more than that, Da. I feel like I've let you and Mommy down. I wanted to prove that Lelands and Thomson and everyone else was wrong and you were right and you had the baseball all along."

Then my father spoke words that truly struck me deep in my heart, "Look, Brian. You have no idea how much happiness you've brought your mother and me just by being yourself again. That is the only thing that's important to us. I don't care about my baseball. You can give it away if you want."

And so we drove on, into the Queens night, and I was already starting to feel better. I had my dad's approval, and that meant the world to me. His unconditional love meant much more to me than finding the Thomson ball. It was mom and dad who got me out of my life of tortured fear and on this path. Maybe the fate of the ball was meant to stay a mystery, but that didn't really matter. I felt that my search was over, and I could live with that. As long as my mom and dad were proud of me, my story would have a happy ending.

The Angel

I spent the next few weeks following Dad's advice. I came up with what I thought was a clever way to tie the story together, focusing on the forensic evidence, the discovery of Helen Gawn's name, and the history of the game. I'd leave the fate of the ball a mystery.

It wouldn't be the first film to end with an unsolved mystery. There had been at least three different documentaries about the "Lost City of Atlantis." This would be more like the "Lost Ball of the Polo Grounds."

In a way, I was happy that the roller-coaster ride was over. It felt great to be back on terra firma. I divided my time between finishing a rough cut of the film, which I was calling *The Shot Heard Around the World* and getting started on a new project. Sal Del Giudice and I got serious about developing that pilot for a baseball reality TV show and a lot of my time was spent trying to secure Darryl Strawberry or Reggie Jackson as our host. Then one day, I got a call that turned my life upside down once again. Brendan was home from school on a holiday break, and he called me one Saturday afternoon and said he had new information about the ball.

I was driving out to Long Island that Saturday anyway so I agreed to meet up with him for a few minutes.

When I got to his place, he was standing out front waiting for me.

Brendan jumped in the car and told me his grandfather had called and said that his neighbor, Robert, had information about the ball.

I rolled my eyes. It seemed to me that after all I'd been through, there was little to no chance my assistant's grandfather's neighbor would be the one to help me find out what happened to the ball. But I humored Brendan and asked what this guy Robert knew.

"I'm not exactly sure. Grandpa said the guy will only talk to you. He's nervous. Actually, Grandpa said he's freaking out."

At this point, I figured the meeting was going to go one of two ways. Maybe the guy was going to be another Simkins telling me he'd discovered the ball was stored in Area 51 next to the original U-2 spy plane and an alien skeleton. Or maybe he was just another baseball freak telling me the *Daily News* had reprinted the wrong game-time temperature from October 3, 1951.

The last thing I needed was the disappointment of yet another lead that went nowhere after I'd already moved on, but in the end I just couldn't resist. A few days later, Brendan and I drove out to Cranford, New Jersey, to meet up with Seymore's buddy Robert.

Driving on the Jersey Turnpike, with not much scenery to look at, I ran the last month of the search over and over in my head. I just couldn't put my finger on anything I could have done differently in finding Helen Gawn. The private detectives did a bang-up job, yet the mystery lady remained just that—a mystery.

We pulled up in front of Seymore's colonial-style home, on a quiet, tree-lined block in suburban New Jersey. Brendan introduced me to Seymore. He was in his early eighties but could have passed for seventy. He shook my hand with a soft, sincere touch.

"Hiya, Brian. Brendan's told me so much about you. Your film sounds so exciting. Do you think you'll find the ball?"

"I'm really not sure at this point," I said, slightly embarrassed. "But we still have a great story either way."

"It could get even better. Did Brendan tell you who's inside?"

I didn't answer and Seymore looked back at me with a strangely confident glare. Not knowing what to expect, I followed Seymore inside the house. Sitting on the living room couch was a very large man with a shaved head and a black mustache. He was in his late forties and wore a dressy black shirt and tinted eyeglasses. This was Robert Pagluca, a neighbor and friend of Seymore's.

After we were all introduced, I just sat there, waiting for something to happen. Apparently, Robert's friend Donald, who was somehow involved in this story, was on his way over to the house too. Brendan finally broke the ice by telling me that Robert was a big Redskins fan. Knowing my love of the Dallas Cowboys, he thought we'd have something to talk about.

I started to get impatient. I didn't see the point in waiting around for this other guy to arrive. I wanted to know the big secret.

"What's going on, fellas? You didn't bring me all the way out to New Jersey to talk about football."

Seymore told Robert to tell me his story. He took his glasses off and began.

"You're making that film about the home-run ball, right," Robert said in his deep Jersey accent.

"That's me."

"I remember reading about it in the newspaper, but I threw the paper out, so I didn't know how to contact you."

"Then I got talking to Seymore the other day, and he mentioned that Brendan was actually working on that film. I couldn't believe what a crazy coincidence that was."

Robert continued in a steady tone. "You're not going to believe this, but I know where that ball's at."

I leaned back in my chair and just kept listening.

"Me and my buddy Donald were at the ShopRite in Nutley, visiting our pal Bob Murphy. Murph cuts meat behind the deli counter and was on his lunch break. So the three of us were standing at the soda machine near the salad bar talking about boxing. We'll talk about sports all day sometimes. We always kid Murph because he's got the same name as that old boxer 'Sailor Bob Murphy.' You ever hear of him?"

I began shifting in my seat, growing impatient. "What does boxing have to do with Bobby Thomson's baseball?" I asked.

Robert's eyes dropped down but he kept talking. "You need to listen to this, OK? So we're at the soda machine, talking about an old boxing match from 1951 between Sailor Bob Murphy and Jake LaMotta. Then, out of nowhere, some old man at the salad bar overhears us talking about sports and gets in on our conversation. He said he remembered how LaMotta took apart Murphy in the seventh round at the Garden. He was a real sports nut. Then the conversation shifted to baseball. The guy brought up the '51 playoff game all on his own. We talk about that for a while, and then he asks us, 'Do you know that we're standing not far from a sports landmark.'"

I reminded Robert that the Polo Grounds was a long way from Nutley, New Jersey. Besides, the stadium was demolished after the Giants moved to San Francisco in 1958.

"Exactly," he said. "That's why I couldn't figure out what the heck the guy was talking about. Then he tells us, 'We're right near the spot where Thomson's ball is.'"

Now he had my full attention. I asked Robert to please remember exactly what the stranger said next. He nodded in agreement, and spoke with precision.

"He told us that Bobby Thomson's Shot Heard 'Round the World baseball is in a Felician convent in Lodi, New Jersey, that it's been there all these years with Sister Helen, the nun who caught it."

Wait a minute. Did he just say Sister *Helen*?

Before I could even get the next syllable out of my mouth, the doorbell rang.

"That must be Donald. He'll tell you."

I needed a second to catch my breath and think. Maybe I'd been hanging around too many cops, but I wanted to interview Donald separately from Robert so I could hear his account of what happened without Robert in the room. My mind was full of questions: What was their motive? Were they looking to collect a reward? Was there really a nun with the same first name as the woman who Tommy Holmes said caught the ball?

I looked out the window and saw a large yellow school bus. Donald was a driver, on a break from work. I asked Brendan to please have Donald wait in the bus while I continued talking with Robert.

Sitting back down across from Robert, I asked him when he, Donald, and Murphy met the ShopRite stranger.

He told me it was seven or eight days ago and that he looked everywhere for the newspaper article to try to contact me.

I asked Robert what was in it for him? His response sounded very honest. He said he had known Brendan since he was a little kid and was really close friends with Seymore, and he just wanted to help.

I asked him what the stranger's name was.

He said he and his pals were in such shock that they didn't even think to ask his name, that it all happened so fast.

"Do you remember what he looked like?" I asked.

"I been back to the ShopRite about a dozen times to see if I'd bump into him, but he's nowhere to be found"

I snapped back, "That's not what I asked you! I want to know what he looked like."

I was confused and agitated. I had been so happy to put all the craziness behind me, and now here I was sitting next to a man with no agenda telling me a story that would fit nicely in a book of fairy tales. But my gut told me he was telling the truth. I felt like Pacino in *Godfather III*: "Just when I thought I was out, they pull me back in."

Robert described the man as short, maybe five seven, with reddish hair, an elderly person with a face full of freckles.

I asked him to tell me what happened next.

"He said his wife was waiting in the car for him and he had to go. But he told us that stuff about the nun with the ball, and we didn't even ask him anything about it. He just blurted it out. It was spooky."

"And you're sure he didn't introduce himself at any point? Would maybe one of the other guys remember?"

"Brian, if you ask me, his name must be Angel, because he appeared out of nowhere and was gone just as quick. And no one's seen him since."

The room went silent. I had goose bumps, and my heart swelled with emotion. I glanced out the window and saw Brendan sitting in the front seat of the bus with Donald.

Seymore and I exchanged glances and headed out to the bus. Donald Byrd is an African American man in his early fifties. He is a native Floridian who moved to New Jersey twenty years ago.

He talked more passionately and enthusiastically than his buddy Robert. Dressed in a Seton Hall baseball cap and checkered, short-sleeve button-down, he wasted no time while telling me what he described as "some sort of miracle" that had happened a week earlier in the ShopRite.

"Did Robert tell you what happened?" he asked

"I'd rather hear the whole story again from you," I said, trying not to appear overanxious.

"Robert and I have been good friends for years. We know each other from the neighborhood. And once a week or so, we go visit our other friend, Murphy, at the ShopRite he works at in Nutley. So we're talking about boxing, then some guy we never seen before starts talking to us about the Shot Heard 'Round the World. I suppose maybe he read that newspaper article or something. Or maybe saw it on TV."

At this point, I didn't think Donald even realized that I was the guy on the news.

"Anyways, he tells us that ball has been hidden away in a Felician convent for all these years by a Sister Helen."

"Donald, I'm confused. Why did that even come up? Did one of you guys ask him if he knew where the ball was?"

He took off his cap and leaned closer in, "No! That's the crazy thing. He just came out and said it. It was just one of those things. You know, you're talking sports and then some other person joins the conversation. But this guy was serious."

"Really? How do you know that?

"What reason would he have to lie about a thing like that? I didn't even know that ball was still missing. That's why it caught me so off guard. It was so crazy."

"And what did this guy look like," I asked.

"He had freckles like an Irish guy. He was an older guy with red hair, medium height."

"Donald, just one last question." I wanted to see if I could trick him. "When the stranger said Sister Grace had the ball, did he say how she got it?"

"Whoa, wait a second. Not Grace. Helen," he emphasized. "The woman who caught the ball was named Sister Helen."

Fervor

Wednesday, October 3, 1951

Thomas Hartman was a first-grader who loved the New York Giants. Young Thomas lived in the middle-class German/Irish neighborhood of Richmond Hill, Queens, with his parents and five siblings. Many days after school, Thomas would ride along on his dad's fruit truck as he made deliveries to neighborhoods like Glendale and Canarsie. The Hartmans were the only family on the block with a TV set, and he watched from the foyer as his uncle Doney, who had been stricken by polio years earlier, was lifted up the concrete steps and into the Hartman house that Wednesday afternoon. Doney and Thomas's father, Herman, were huge Giants fans too, and there was no way they weren't going to watch the deciding playoff game together. Throughout the afternoon, they yelled taunts at the screen when things went well for the Giants, shouting, "The Giants are going to the World Series tomorrow!" or "Dem Bums are going to lose!"

Thomas started uttering the same phrases, trying to be like one of the grown-ups. But the room grew quiet in the eighth inning, when the Dodgers opened up a big lead. Herman somehow remained hopeful and kept reminding his son to keep the faith. He told him, "Son, it's been an up-and-down season, and these men never gave up, and they won't give up now. I know what they are capable of."

Thomas listened to his dad and prayed for a miraculous comeback. With each hit in the ninth inning, his hopes rose more and more. It was working! His faith was being rewarded. After Thomson hit the game-winning home run, Thomas's life changed in ways no one could have imagined. After seeing what positive thinking and having faith in the impossible could bring, he became a very spiritual person and eventually went into the priesthood. Many years later, he would recall the impact of seeing the home run: "After Bobby hit it, something was born in me—faith. That moment as a young child gave me the security to believe in God and allowed me to seek a higher order as a priest."

I WAS DESPERATE to try to make sense of the incredible information Robert and Donald had just given me. I had two major questions: Could Sister Helen be the same person as the Helen Gawn whom Tommy Holmes wrote about? And who was this mysterious stranger who talked to Robert and Donald in Shop Rite, anyway? My first instinct was to get back in the car and drive straight to Lodi, but I headed back to New York to regroup. For the first time in months I felt like I was destined to solve this mystery. Robert and Donald were just the latest in a string of tiny miracles that were all bringing me toward this baseball.

From the beginning, it never made sense to me that someone, especially a baseball fan, would have this ball and not know it. I still have a ball that Wally Backman fouled off in 1987, and that's no Shot Heard 'Round the World. But if a nun had had the ball hidden away in her convent for all these years, then no wonder nobody ever found it. No one would even know to look there. That's a theory I could buy into.

With Joey and Greg off the payroll, it was time for me to step in as detective now. It was not that different from what I had been doing all along, so I embraced the challenge. In my hunt for the ball, I had started with next to nothing. Now I had a name, I had a picture, I even had a last known location. How hard could it possibly be to solve the rest of the mystery? I was about to find out.

First thing Monday morning, I got into the editing room, which had become my own private office by this point, and I called the convent in Lodi, asking for the mother superior. I learned that her name was Sister Virginia, and was told try again later. I finally got her on the phone the third time I called back. After I introduced myself, I got right to the point.

"I'm a filmmaker working on a project that I believe you could be a great help with."

In a monotone, she asked, "Is this a student film? Because I'm not connected with that part of the college."

She was talking about Felician College. The school and the convent were located on the same campus, and apparently people often confused them.

"Sister, I'm not a student. I am an independent filmmaker, and I'm making a documentary about a famous baseball that's been missing since 1951. I have reason to believe that the ball might be in your convent."

I closed my eyes and waited for her response. She remained silent, so I continued.

"I know this may sound very strange, but is there a nun there named Sister Helen Gawn? It's possible she may be in possession of a very rare and valuable baseball."

She asked if this was a prank call. After hearing some of the crazies call in after the media blitz, I could empathize. I assured her I was on the level and gave her a brief explanation of what I was trying to accomplish. She told me she couldn't help, but I wasn't ready to give up.

"Can I just ask you one question? Is there a sister named Helen in your convent?"

Sister Helen (*top*), dressed in secular clothes, watches the ball land in the stands near her.

She didn't even want to answer that, simply saying, "We don't usually give out that kind of information."

It almost felt like some sort of cover-up. Her tone was slightly dismissive, and I was confused. I thought nuns were supposed to help people, so I tried again.

"Sister, I'm begging you. This means more to me than I can even explain."

A long pause, then, "Well, I might be able to help with something."

It was a classic case of good news, bad news. Sister Virginia had been in the Lodi convent since the start of her days teaching at Felician College fifty-five years ago. She had a remarkable memory. She said she knew practically every Felician sister in the Northeast. No Sister Helen ever lived in her convent. But the good news was that she did recall a Felician sister named Helen in the fifties, who lived in either the Connecticut or Buffalo convent.

I asked her if she remembered anything at all about this Sister Helen.

"Well, she had a reputation for being a little aggressive for this particular order of the church, slightly rebellious you might say, but this was a long time ago."

She went on to explain that she and Helen crossed paths once or twice, and she described her as a very tall, thin woman with short, wavy brown hair. Even though *Pafko at the Wall* was a bit grainy and you couldn't see the full body of the only woman in the area where the ball landed, you could see her face, and indeed, that's what her hair looked like. Also, she had to be tall to be able to stick out from the men surrounding her. For all I knew, this Sister Helen could be alive and well in Buffalo, sleeping with the Thomson ball next to her on her night table alongside a print of Psalm 23.

I pleaded with Sister Virginia to let me come to the convent to meet with her. I wanted to get her on film and see if she remembered anything else about Sister Helen. I also wanted to enlist her help in reaching out to the other Felician convents to see if they could help me find out what happened to Helen and the ball. But Sister Virginia was either unable or unwilling to help, "Good luck, but I'm sorry. I've already told you everything I know."

I sensed something was amiss. I decided to put a film crew together and drive out to Lodi to try to meet with Sister Virginia in person. Maybe when she saw the lengths to which I was willing to go, she'd choose to help me.

The place was easy to find. I really didn't know what to expect, but I went prepared. I brought *Pafko at the Wall* to show Sister Virginia, hoping she'd be more cooperative in person than she was on the telephone. I wanted to see if she'd recognize the lady I suspected to be Helen—they had met, after all.

The convent was situated behind a small campus, which sat

on a two-way road in Lodi, a quiet town. There were big, beautiful trees swaying in the wind out front and several religious ornaments—statues of Jesus, Mother Mary, and various styles of crosses, including one large white one on the top of the main building out front.

Before attempting to see Sister Virginia, I wanted to get an establishing shot of the convent, but I couldn't find a high enough spot to set up the camera. Looking around, I noticed there was a private house directly across the road, which would give me a perfect view. I told Brendan to keep a watch out, while I climbed the fire escape and then pulled myself up onto the roof. Sure, I was trespassing. But the shot was going to be perfect!

I asked Brendan to hoist the camera up to me. Before he could, he told me to look across the road. Three or four nuns had congregated in front of the convent about two hundred yards from where I was perched on the roof. Before I even had a chance to turn on the camera, a Jersey state trooper pulled up in his patrol car. The nuns had ratted me out.

The state trooper ordered me to climb down, and told me I was on private property. He pointed to the license plates on our vehicles and said in a powerful voice, "We got a call that some New Yorkers were here with cameras. You want to tell me what business you have with the church?"

I narrowly avoided getting arrested by making up a story about needing some religious imagery for a website we were going to launch. I could see the guys on the crew laughing under their breath in the background. But it worked.

"Just get in your cars and go back where you came from, and we won't have a problem. But don't let me see you around here again."

He didn't need to tell us twice. I knew I needed to try to find some inroads at the Buffalo and Connecticut Felician convents. But before I did, I wanted to get some background information on the practices of the Felician Sisters. Maybe if I learned more about who they are and how they operate, I would have more success in enlisting their help.

Enter Monsignor Thomas Hartman. Hartman is a well-known theologian and also a television and radio personality. I had heard Father Tom on the *Imus in the Morning* radio show a few times. I'd also seen him on his own local TV show, *The God Squad,* which Father Hartman has cohosted, along with Rabbi Marc Gellman, since 1988 on the Telecare network.

I knew he had a long history of explaining sacred practices to people in the secular world. I also knew he was a sports fan—he was the team chaplain for the New York Jets. He was proud of having baptized Jets quarterback Vinny Testaverde's baby.

Hartman agreed to meet me in his church in Hicksville, Long Island. Father Tom suffers from Parkinson's Disease and was very kind to spend some time with me on a Friday afternoon while he prepared his Sunday sermon. I was greeted at the front of the church by his assistant, Omar, and taken straight up to Father Tom's private living quarters. I was impressed when I walked into the living area and saw a framed and autographed picture of Willie Mays on a wall above a Mays signed baseball on Father Tom's desk. I felt the gentle hand of fate on my shoulder once again: It turned out Father Tom was an old-time New York Giants fan and was seven years old when Thomson launched his big home run.

We rode the elevator down to the main level, where Father Tom's church is located. Along the way, he told me he was a pitcher in high school for the Pius X Catholic school in Uniondale, New York. I was tempted to ask him about some sports stories but was sensitive to his physical condition and didn't want to take more time than I needed.

We entered the small but elegant church on the main floor. Father Tom, a handsome man with shiny white hair, was dressed in his black priest attire and sat in a big red velvet chair that Omar set up for him. I was across from him in the first row of the church pews. He walked me through what he knew about the Felician Sisters.

The order was started in Poland many centuries ago. The Felician sisters take vows of poverty, chastity, and silence. Their emblem is a flaming torch. Very few sisters who join the order ever leave. Hartman explained that most of the sisters were in their eighties and some even in their nineties. There are only 1,400 sisters worldwide.

When I told Father Tom that I believed a nun in the Felician order was in possession of Bobby Thomson's baseball, he was intrigued.

"That might explain why no one has come forward with it all these years. Privacy is very important to the Felician sisters." He told me about a lunch he once had with Mother Teresa, and how she explained the importance of religious people leading lives outside the public spotlight.

Then I asked him a question that had been on my mind: "Take a look at this picture, Father. It shows a woman I believe is Sister Helen, but she's not wearing her habit. Would she have been allowed to leave the convent without her habit?"

He suggested that she wouldn't have worn her habit to the game because she would have wanted to blend in with the crowd.

"Brian, in order for this sister to attend a baseball game, especially in the 1950s, it's likely she would have to have broken a few rules. But I know firsthand that baseball could make a person do that," he smiled.

When I showed the photo to Father Tom, he pointed directly to her. He observed that her hair was cut in the style that a sister would have worn and said, "When you have been in the church as long as I have, you get a sense of what a nun looks like. This sister looks like a person who lived her life with fervor."

I felt I was on to something. If Helen had broken the strict rules of the convent and wasn't supposed to be at the game, she certainly wouldn't have wanted anyone to know she had the ball. Finally, I had a plausible explanation as to why the fate of the ball had remained a mystery all these years.

SIXTEEN

The Three Helens

It was clear to me that there was something larger than life at work by this point. I was nearly convinced after my conversation with Monsignor Hartman that a Felician nun, dressed in secular clothing, had somehow made her way into the Polo Grounds and caught the ball that day. Irving's claim that he saw a woman walking *away* from Tommy Holmes even made sense. She would have wanted to elude his questions enough to keep her identity hidden from the church. She wouldn't have wanted a front-page headline in the next day's *Brooklyn Daily Eagle* reading: THE NUN AND THE BASEBALL. She wasn't even supposed to be there.

If Helen wanted to avoid scrutiny, it seemed to me that the last place she'd end up would be the Giants' clubhouse, asking the team to sign the ball. This left me having to explain to my dad that it was now almost certain that his ball was not the Thomson ball.

I wasn't exactly sure yet how to connect all the dots, but I *was* sure of one thing: I needed to have a heart-to-heart talk with him. It had been a long, emotional journey for both of us, and he needed to know what I knew.

On my way home from my talk with Monsignor Hartman I went to see him. He was not far away, in Syosset, Long Island, watching my niece Melissa's high school softball game. It was only a fifteen-minute drive, but I decided to wait at my sister's house for him to return from the ball field.

When I heard his car pull into the garage, my heart started to pound. He walked in the house and asked with a playful smirk, "You find the phantom of the Polo Grounds yet?" I kept a straight face. I had to admit it was a good line, but I was not in a light-hearted mood. By now I knew he was going to resist whatever I told him about Sister Helen.

I challenged him to a game of pool. He and Uncle Heshie used to shoot pool all the time at the New Lots Avenue Pool Hall in Brooklyn, where reputed members of Murder, Inc., founded by Meyer Lansky and Bugsy Siegel, once racked 'em up. He couldn't resist the offer.

Playing with him always made me think of the times back in the day when we'd played bumper pool in the basement of cousin Marlon the Bookie's house on those glorious Sundays, as Marlon sweated out NFL games piped in from that gigantic satellite dish.

Leaning over to break the rack, Dad said with a knowing glance, "So what's so important that you drove all the way out here to tell me?"

The balls scattered across the red felt, and it was my turn to shoot. I circled the table, pulled back my cue, and drilled the thirteen ball into the leather-mesh corner pocket. Dad continued in his deliberate tone, "What, do you think I'm stupid? Just remember, I made you. I know what you're thinking before you do. So, come on. Spill the beans."

Leaning my pool stick against the side of the table, I said, "Poppa, at the diner, I told you I thought a woman named Helen Gawn caught the ball . . ."

Dad nodded his head and chimed in. "And the overpaid private dicks came up with zilch."

"Uh, yeah. Well, I think I really know what happened to the ball now."

He paced back and forth near the pool table, stick in hand, eyeballing me.

"Dad, I'm serious. Please just listen without jumping down my throat. Then you can say whatever you like."

I shared the whole Sister Helen story with him from top to bottom. He looked at me blankly. It was better than the way everyone else looked at me eighteen months ago when I first told them I was going to uncover the mystery behind the missing baseball.

But I wasn't telling this incredible story to a sportscaster or museum curator. This was my dad! And even though I believed in my heart what he told me driving home from Shea, I knew he really did have a lot riding on this and couldn't help but react straight from the gut.

"You expect me to believe that some *nun* has the baseball and I don't," he said. "Are you crazy?!"

I let him blow off steam, knowing he wasn't ready to accept this. Instead, he started bombarding me with questions . . . some of them sarcastic.

"Who is she? What does she look like? Is she still alive? Where is the ball? Did she give it to Jesus? Tell me, did she also find Babe Ruth's sixtieth home-run ball from 1927 under the Red Sea when Moses parted it? Come on, give me a break!"

I softly explained to him that Sister Helen having the baseball all these years really made a lot of sense, especially given Father Hartman's point about how it explained why the ball had never been found. Dad swayed back and forth thinking it all through. I asked him to have a seat so we could talk it out.

I put my arm around his shoulder, and together we walked to the couch that looked out over the swimming pool. The water was calm and the sun formed a tiny rainbow around it. I tried again to slowly explain the situation, step by step. Seymore calling Brendan, the stranger in the ShopRite talking to Robert and Donald, Sister Virginia admitting there was a rebellious nun named Helen, and then Father Tom explaining why it might all be kept a secret. The only part that didn't make sense now was the last name—G-A-W-N.

My dad's look softened. "Do you really believe a nun has the ball, Brian?"

"I do, Poppa. I really do. It explains everything."

"I don't know . . . ," he began, but his voice trailed off.

I desperately needed his approval and asked him how it would make him feel if I was able to somehow prove this. I explained that without him on my side, I didn't think I could move forward.

I meant every word. Leaning back on the couch, he took a long breath. His eyes locked with mine and he said the words I never thought I would hear him say: "If you could prove it one hundred and one percent to me, I may concede."

Then he repeated, with a vulnerability I had never heard before in his voice, "I may concede that I don't have the real ball."

My dad is not one to concede anything so I didn't really know what to think. I was worried about him.

"But, Dad, how would that honestly make you feel?"

"In my heart I would feel good for you," he said, "because you've been on this journey for so long, and of course I would like to see you succeed. On the other hand, I'd feel lousy for me because I really thought I had the ball."

Jack and Sandy Biegel at granddaughter Samara's bat mitzvah in 2006.
From the author's collection

His eyes locked on mine once again, and he continued, "If you feel she truly has the ball, then you have my blessing. Brian, remember: I created you. You live inside of me. I want you to finish out this mission. You need to keep moving forward on your quest. I love you no matter what happens. Go find her."

We stood up from the couch and embraced in a hug. This was the last bit of incentive I needed. I was so close now to finding the truth that I knew nothing could stop me.

THE NEXT DAY, I knew exactly what I had to do. Sister Virginia, the mother superior from Lodi, had mentioned to me that Sister

Helen was from the Felician convent in either Buffalo or Connecticut. I needed to call both of those places and ask more information about who Helen was and also to find a way to resolve the Gawn issue.

After several calls to both convents, I began to get frustrated. Each time, a different nun answered the phone, and none of them was willing to help me. My calls were met with confusion—the general assumption seemed to be that I was a telemarketer at best or a lunatic at worst.

The pressure was really starting to mount. I had finally resolved the concerns with my dad, but now I was catching flack from my partners on the film. Frankly, I saw their point. They had been patient until now, but then were losing faith in the new direction of the project. They didn't feel that I'd be able to prove the nun theory because I didn't have any conclusive information and I wasn't getting anywhere with the Felician convents. I still felt I could pull it off if I had more time, but I couldn't justify keeping the production up and running anymore. "Brian, you're chasing a ghost," was a common refrain.

I decided to keep at the search on my own. We put the editing process on hold, and I became a one-man show. There were no hard feelings. It was just business. At this point, I really didn't care anyway. I had one goal, and it wasn't about making money by selling a film.

Six weeks went by with no progress, and I was more nervous than ever. Here I was, with the ball so close I could practically smell the old red stitching, and I was up against an unbreakable force—stubborn Felician nuns. I was back where I was before I met Robert and Donald—ready to give up.

One night my mom overheard me arguing with my brother on the phone. He was lobbying for me to just finish up the film with what I had, even if it meant leaving the Sister Helen stuff on the cutting-room floor. His other idea was that I just keep calling the convents until I got somewhere. Steve has always been a great source of support for me, but he was not understanding my current predicament.

"Steve, you don't understand!" I yelled into the phone. "Every time I call the convent, a different nun answers the phone. The second I say the word "baseball," they think I'm a ticket broker or something. You just have no idea how difficult it is to penetrate their walls."

He suggested that I stop calling and just go directly to the convent to speak to them in person.

"Are you going to bail me out of jail?" I snapped back at him. "I almost got arrested the last time I tried to just show up."

My mom, who was sitting in her favorite armchair in the living room, had been watching me pace all around the house talking frantically into my cell phone. After I hung up, she waited for me to calm down, then delivered the same sort of smart and practical advice she had given me from day one.

"Why don't you try a different approach when calling the nuns. Maybe mention that you are interested in making a donation—a large donation. But to do so, you need to find this baseball."

I was planning on giving some money to the sisters anyway if the ball turned up, but it hadn't occurred to me to mention the potential economic windfall to any of the nuns. My mom's idea made sense: Though they took personal vows of poverty, they could certainly use the money for the various charities they supported.

Energized by Mom's advice, I picked up right where I left off. And her advice paid big dividends, almost right away. When I made my next call to the Buffalo convent, a sister named Felicia answered the telephone. In all the calls I'd made there, she and

I hadn't spoken before. I asked her about this, and she told me it was because she normally never answered the phone—she was only covering for a friend who was sick. She listened to what I had to say and was pleasant, friendly, and engaging. I mentioned the idea of making a donation to the Felician convent if I found the baseball. She must have heard the relief in my voice.

She assured me that she'd help in any way she could.

Then I asked the big question: Had she ever heard of a Felician nun named Sister Helen?

There was a slight pause. My mouth went dry.

Yes. She knew of a Sister Helen from a very long time ago when Felicia had first joined the order.

After I asked her to describe Sister Helen, Felicia said that even though it was many years ago, she remembered a woman very tall and slender. I asked her about Helen's hair. She told me the few times she saw Sister Helen without her habit she had beautiful, wavy brown hair cut short.

When I asked if there was anything curious or different about her, the response sent butterflies into my stomach.

"She was an avid baseball fan. She'd listen to games on the radio," Sister Felicia replied.

There they were—two key pieces of the puzzle. The physical description matched, and she was a *baseball* fan! The mother superior in Lodi said that Helen was rebellious. She wouldn't elaborate, but I imagined that what she meant was that Helen was never quite able to devote herself fully to religious matters. I thought about how much the game must have meant to her, as a connection to her old life and the outside world. So many of the people I'd met during this process had viewed their lives through the prism of baseball. Maybe Sister Helen was another whose life was in some way shaped by baseball. I wasn't even born when this game took place, and yet it was affecting me profoundly—bringing me from the depths of mental debilitation to the heights of rediscovering myself.

Sister Felicia also remembered that Helen moved out of the Buffalo Province a few years later, maybe to New Mexico, the West Coast charter convent. Then I asked Sister Felicia if she knew Sister Helen's last name. She did not, but she put me on hold to check. I sat on the edge of my seat with my eyes closed for nearly five minutes. I wanted her to tell me that Helen's last name was Gawn.

"Mr. Biegel, Helen's last name was Hojnacki."

I asked her to please double check. She read it again. "Her name was Sister Helen Hojnacki. She left our convent in 1953. Doesn't say where she went. But in the notes section, it says 'possible relocation west—to California or New Mexico.'"

I was deflated and very confused. It seemed like too much of a coincidence that Sister Helen Hojnacki was a baseball fan who looked just like the woman in the picture. But why did she have the wrong name? At least I still had a trail to follow. I called the convent in New Mexico and asked to speak to the mother superior, saying that Sister Felicia from the Buffalo convent had told me to call. After leaving several messages, I finally got a call back from Sister Seraphine.

She told me that she had had a sister named Helen in her province from the late fifties to the end of her life in 1990, but her name was Sister Helen Rita, not Hojnacki.

Now I had three different names for Sister Helen: Gawn, Hojnacki, and Rita. My gut told me that the three women were really all the same person, but there was still the matter of tying it all together.

I explained the whole situation to Sister Seraphine, including the possible donation. She agreed to search through every document they had on record and contact me as soon as she got them all together. I also asked her to try to locate any photos she might have of Sister Helen Rita through the years, preferably one from the 1950s.

I had in the back of my mind the idea that the ball might still be somewhere within the convent walls. "Let me ask you something: Is there a possibility that any of Sister Helen's old possessions might still be in storage somewhere at the convent?"

"I'm afraid not. When a sister passes on, her worldly possessions are returned to her family."

That meant the ball—if she'd ever had it—was most likely with one of Helen's relatives. Maybe I'd catch a break and that information would be in the paperwork that Sister Seraphine was digging up for me. While I waited for her to check the old convent records, which she warned me would take a few weeks, I went to talk to Father Hartman again, hoping he could help explain the three names.

I returned to the same chapel where I'd met with Father Tom the first time. Omar had already escorted him down into the church to meet with a troubled young boy who was there with his mom. I stood silently in the background and watched them pray together. After the boy and his mom left, Omar signaled me to approach Monsignor Hartman, who greeted me with a warm smile.

I explained to Father Tom about the three Helens, and he quickly shed light on the situation.

"Remember, if a Felician nun from Buffalo was at a baseball game in Manhattan in 1951, she would have had to break a few rules to get there."

It then hit me that she gave Tommy Holmes a fake last name to protect her identity. As for the change from Hojnacki to Rita, Hartman didn't seem surprised at all.

"In the fifties, Catholic nuns were allowed to change their names when they renewed their vows. Sometimes they did this when they reached a certain status in religious life, and sometimes they did this when they moved from one location to another."

"What would influence a nun to take a particular name?" I asked him.

"New names weren't chosen at random," he explained. "A nun might take on the name of a saint whom they felt a personal connection to in their religious or spiritual lives."

I had to admit I wasn't too up on the background of the saints, so I once again looked to Father Tom for help. "Who was Saint Rita?"

"If a nun took the name of Saint Rita, it would have been to honor the patron saint of achieving the impossible."

The patron saint of achieving the impossible. What better saint for Sister Helen Hojnacki to honor! Maybe she changed her name to honor the impossible achievement that recently occurred in her beloved sport of baseball—the Shot Heard 'Round the World.

I wanted to learn more, so I dug deep into the history of Saint Rita and found a remarkable connection. But rather than just rely on information from various websites and books, I wanted to hear the story firsthand from someone who knew it well. Searching through the list of new contacts I had made, I recalled that Lolita Lopez was originally from Texas and started her career covering baseball down there.

I remembered a brief conversation I had had several months earlier with Lolita when I met her up at the WB11 TV studio with Sal Marchiano. Having been raised in the Lone Star State, she had a working knowledge of all things relating to sports in Texas.

I contacted Lolita and asked if she could call in a favor and allow me to talk with her inside Shea Stadium. I hadn't been back there since that dreadful night I had the panic attack.

Lolita pulled some strings, and soon after, I was soaking up the sight of the bright green grass in front of the orange-and-blue stadium seats on a sunny, early-spring afternoon. Lolita stood on the top step of the Mets's dugout and talked to me as I sat on the cushioned Mets's dugout bench. She explained to me that her first reporter's job was down in south Texas.

"I remember a lot of the high school and college baseball players used to wear a medallion around their neck for good luck," she explained. "One day I asked one of them, 'What is that for?' Surprisingly enough, it was a medallion of Saint Rita, the patron saint of achieving the impossible."

She went on to tell the rest of the story. Back in 1921, in Big Lake, Texas, two Catholic nuns invested in an oil well. This was allowed by their priest on one condition: He told them to baptize a rose, and sprinkle the petals in the oil well, and pray every day to Saint Rita for luck—to achieve the impossible and strike oil.

During the downtime from drilling, the workers built a baseball field near the rig. After seventeen months of digging and drilling, they still came up dry. The nuns didn't have much money left to pay the workers, but they decided to give it one more month. In the eighteenth and final month, they finally hit a gusher.

The nuns named the oil well the Santa Rita. Because of the baseball field that was built nearby and the commitment the workers had to the game (one of the men, Snipe Connelly, went on to play in the big leagues), the Santa Rita oil well became forever synonymous with baseball. In fact, many of the Saint Rita medallions have an engraving of a man swinging a baseball bat on the back side—forever connecting the story of Santa Rita and baseball. To this day, high school and college baseball players in Texas and New Mexico wear the Saint Rita medallion for good luck.

I can't say I was surprised by this story. After all that had happened on my search, the word *surprise* didn't really have meaning for me anymore. Now it *really* made sense why Sister Helen would have taken that particular name.

As the sun shone down from high above, I asked Lolita if she thought it was reasonable to think that a nun who loved baseball would take the name Rita when renewing her vows.

"I think it's most definitely possible that a nun would change her name to Rita if she loved the game. The two are linked forever. There's only *one* saint in the world that has any connection whatso ever with the game of baseball—that's Saint Rita."

SEVENTEEN

Digging Up the Past

When I finally heard back from Sister Seraphine, she told me that she had spoken to a former mother superior of Helen's from her years in New Mexico, Sister Patricia. Patricia confirmed that Helen was an avid baseball fan and used to listen to games on the radio in her room. She also told me she was going to FedEx copies of all of Sister Helen's information, including several photos of her from her days in the convent. The Felician Sisters were fully on board.

The envelope arrived on a Tuesday morning. I opened it to find four typewritten documents printed on plain white paper. Two pages looked like transfer applications, full of personal information. The other two looked like a résumé of sorts, giving the years and locations where Helen had lived and worked.

This is what I learned: Helen Hojnacki was born in Syracuse, New York, on October 22, 1914. This means that she would have been thirty-six years old on the day of the game, roughly the age the woman in *Pafko at the Wall* appears to be. She entered religious life on July 2, 1932, in Tonawanda, New York. She spent most of the next two decades living and teaching in various parts of western New York. But from 1950 to 1952, she was a member of the Felician Sisters in Buffalo, New York. So the time frame was correct—she definitely lived in New York State on October 3, 1951. I learned that from there, she lived in two more western New York locales, Batavia and Olean, and taught at several Catholic schools until 1960. That's when she arrived in the Felician Sisters' charter convent in Rio Rancho, New Mexico, as Sister Helen Rita. There was no specific information as to when exactly her name was changed. Even with all I had discovered, I realized, looking back, that maybe some of my questions just weren't meant to be answered.

From 1960 on, New Mexico was her home base, but she continued to travel, teaching French and religious studies in various Catholic schools in Pomona, Claremont, and Monterey, California. She would teach for a semester or two in California, where her parents lived, then spend summers, holidays, and long retreats in New Mexico. One odd fact: Helen's father passed away on October 3, 1974, twenty-three years to the day after the Thomson game.

Sister Helen died on April 14, 1990, in Pomona, California. Her body was shipped to Albuquerque, New Mexico, where she was buried near the Rio Rancho convent alongside the other Felician sisters based in New Mexico.

In addition to the documents, Sister Seraphine sent me three photos of Helen. One was from the early 1960s, a decade after the game. The others were from the mid to late 1970s. There was a resemblance between the nun in the three photos and the woman in the stands, enough to give me hope but nothing conclusive.

There was one other piece of useful information in the file: Sister Helen's emergency contact information, which contained a phone number and an address in California where her family moved. The number on the application was "Monterey Frontier 5-3703." I tried all the area codes in California using that exchange but had no luck. They were all either wrong numbers or disconnected lines.

I briefly considered calling Joey and Greg again but decided to go in another direction. I reached out to the man who was willing to help my dad take on Lelands in the beginning—Larry Rosen. Somewhere along the line, I had learned that Rosen, a high-powered attorney, had access to databases that might be able to help. I explained my predicament to Larry, and he agreed to help out on a pro bono basis as a favor to me *and* my dad. I gave Larry the names of Helen's two biological sisters that I got from the documents—Charlotte and Genevieve. There was a single address listed as the last known residence for both of them in Carmel, California.

Rosen came up huge in his research. Through bank mortgage statements, he discovered that Genevieve lived in New York City in 1951. Buffalo is a long way from the Polo Grounds, but now I had a New York City connection. Genevieve had passed away several years ago, but she had two sons—John and Paul. Rosen found a phone number and address for Paul in Las Vegas.

With no cameraman, sound person, or any other outside help, I mounted a Panasonic AG-DVX100 camera on a tripod in an empty office and filmed myself calling him at the number Larry provided. He picked up the phone on the second ring, and I launched into my story. He accused me of being a prank caller and hung up. I called back right away, thinking maybe I could leave him a message that might get through to him. To my surprise, he picked up again.

"Paul, please don't hang up," I said, trying not to sound too desperate.

"I don't collect baseball memorabilia. Why are you calling me?" he barked.

Before he could hang up again, I quickly mentioned that I knew his mom's name was Genevieve and I had his attention.

As I spoke, Paul relaxed. He revealed that he had known his aunt Helen fairly well. He had even visited her at the Buffalo convent a couple of times when he was little. He said the thing that stuck out most about her in his hazy memory was that she was a strong-willed person. He told me that she moved around from convent to convent and school to school so often because she liked to do things her own way and was not always happy with the rules and teaching practices at her various residences—just the sort of person to ignore the rules and steal away for a baseball game, I thought. He confirmed for me that in 1951, he and his parents had lived in Manhattan. He didn't remember the address, but it was in a "big skyscraper uptown." His family moved around a lot because of his father's job, and they were in New York City for only four or five years.

At first he laughed at the idea that his aunt had caught the Thomson ball. But as he thought about it, the idea took root with him.

"If she had caught the ball, she would have to have kept it a secret because of the strict rules of the convent," he explained. "If she hadn't told the truth to her mother superior about going to New York City to be at the game, that would have been a tremendous sin."

"Is there anyone else she might have told? Your mom maybe?" I asked.

"I wouldn't be surprised if she kept it to herself, telling it only to the priest in confession."

I asked him how he thought it would have been possible for her to get to the game in the first place. He told me that anything was possible with Helen, that she traveled all over the place.

Paul had been only six in 1951 and couldn't remember if his aunt Helen stayed in their uptown apartment for one night in October all those years ago. It was all making sense now. She could have pulled this off with only two people knowing—Genevieve and Genevieve's husband.

"If Sister Helen told my mom a secret, especially of her own personal shame, then Mom would not have told anyone. My mom and dad were pretty religious people, so if she asked them not to say anything, they would have taken that secret to the grave."

Then I asked the next big question. "What happened to Helen's belongings after she passed away?"

He explained that Genevieve had been given a shoebox from the sisters in New Mexico at the cemetery. Inside it were Helen's worldly belongings. With my heart pounding, I stood up and asked Paul the biggest question of all.

"Do you have any idea what was in that shoebox?"

"Mom never let anyone look inside. Only she knew."

"Paul, what happened to the shoebox?"

"After the funeral, we drove back to California, and Mom opened up the car window and hurled the shoebox into a landfill in Monterey."

It's Not About the Ball

I t took me a few days to process what I had just learned. I knew from Sister Seraphine that Helen's possessions all went back to her family after she passed away. Those possessions were tossed into a landfill in California seventeen years ago. One of the guys working at Heavy Light asked me if I was going to try to dig it up. He was serious. He suggested I hire a construction company to bulldoze tons of dirt to look for the buried shoebox. This was the moment when I knew that finding the actual ball just wasn't going to happen. This was a stunning defeat.

I moped around the house for the next couple of days, not yet ready to tell my parents what I'd learned, but they knew there was a problem. In time, I eventually opened up to them.

The kitchen in our house had always been like our sanctuary—even as kids growing up. It wasn't large but held enough memories—good and bad—to fill a stadium. The three of us were having our traditional Sunday breakfast—bagels, lox, and cream cheese. The raw onion Dad put on his bagel was so strong, it made my eyes tear from across the table. I raised a napkin to my eye. Then my mom tried to lighten my somber mood by joking, "It's fine, baby. No need to cry."

I just blurted it out. "I think the ball was thrown into a landfill in California."

Neither of them reacted.

"Did you guys hear me? I spoke to Helen's nephew. He said his mom threw Helen's worldly belongings into a freakin' dump in Monterey. They were in a shoebox."

They just listened as I told them that this spelled the end of any hope anyone ever had of finding the ball. But they were hardly fazed. Especially my dad.

"So you're just going to give up?"

"What do you want me to do? Hire a team of bulldozers to dig up a thousand tons of dirt to look for a shoebox?!"

Dad looked forcefully at me. "It's not about the baseball anymore, Brian."

"Then what's it about, Dad?"

"It's about the truth."

I couldn't believe I was hearing this. Of all people, my *dad* was telling me it wasn't about the baseball. My mom agreed with my father. I again asked just what the hell I was supposed to do.

"Your father just said it. Explain the truth."

Then Dad fixed me with an intense glare—the one that had always meant he wasn't playing around. "Your job's not done yet, champ," he said. "You came this far. Now go finish the goddamn thing!"

I realized he was right. Maybe I wouldn't be able to find the Thomson ball, but I could still prove beyond a reasonable doubt that Sister Helen was the one who ended up with it. I remembered something that Hal Sherman had told me over a year ago. It was just one sentence, but it was never far from my mind. Pointing to *Pafko at the Wall* at Taka Labs, he had said, "The answers are in this photo."

The forensic approach to photography yielded much success the first time around, and I hoped I could employ the same strategy to connect the nun with the lady in the stands. I talked to detectives Sherman and Austin about getting involved in the project again. Sherman was deep into a consulting gig for the FBI, but Austin was eager to get back in the game. But when I told him exactly what I was looking for—to match a woman in two separate photos taken approximately a decade apart—he recommended a forensic sketch artist named Stephen Mancusi.

Before contacting Mancusi, I did a little background check. He had quite a reputation. I found articles about him in several places, including the *Daily News,* the *London Sunday Telegraph,* and the *New York Times.* He had also appeared on shows like ABC's *20/20,* NBC's *Unsolved Mysteries,* and CBS's *Good Morning America.*

Mancusi was the senior forensic artist for the NYPD and had more than two decades of experience in solving high-profile crimes. It was Mancusi's composite drawing in 2002 of the infamous Stuyvesant Town rapist that appeared on the front cover of the *New York Daily News* and eventually led to the capture and conviction of the perpetrator. Mancusi was a detective, first grade, and an expert at comparative facial analysis. The backbone of his work involved measuring the distances between features on a face in separate photos and determining if they belonged to the same person. He was absolutely the perfect man for the job.

DETECTIVE MANCUSI WORKED at One Police Plaza, but we both agreed that it would be better if he conducted his computerized facial analysis from his private art studio in Peekskill, New York. I drove seventy-five minutes to meet him there. Walking up the stairs to his studio, I was suddenly terrified about having Mancusi do the facial comparison. If it went the wrong way, if he could show me definitively that the woman in *Pafko* was not Sister Helen Rita, then my whole theory would be out the window. Maybe I should have just left well enough alone and finished up the film. But no, my journey had never been about trying to find any personal glory; it was only about finding the truth and getting myself back into a world where promise and hope had been restored.

Mancusi was about six feet tall and muscular. He had a shaved head, a white mustache, and large, well-manicured hands. He spoke directly and, in the beginning at least, had a slightly intimidating manner. As we entered his studio he told me, "I usually get paid for this kind of work . . ." I explained to him, as I had already done on the phone, that if I paid him, it created a potential conflict of interest. People might think he was just telling me what I wanted to hear for the money. He was willing to help but wasn't very intrigued by the history of game.

He brought up the images I had sent over to him, one by one, on his computer screen. There were four in all: three of Sister Helen from her time in the convent and a blown-up version of the lady in *Pafko at the Wall*. He began walking me through the results of the three-day analysis he had performed. The first thing he did was to point out the proportional aspects of the face. In other words, the distance between her eyes, the space between her nose and bottom of her chin, where the hairline sat, and the space between the top of her head to the bottom of her chin. These all matched up perfectly.

Next was the shape of her jowls. Mancusi determined through a digital overlay that Helen's jowls had exactly the same depth as

The facial comparative analysis of the lady in the stands (*upper left*) is consistent with the aging Sister Helen Rita (other three). *Photography courtesy of Stephen Mancusi*

those of the lady in the stands. Things were looking promising. Mancusi remarked how both noses had a downward hook and how the height of the cheekbones in all the photos was identical. The high probability that it was the same woman got higher when Mancusi remarked, "There is a very distinctive shape to the face."

I asked him to show me exactly what he meant. Using a red arrow on his screen, he began to point out the unique shape of her face. "Both women have an oval-shaped face with high cheekbones, which don't change as you age. The structure of the skull determines where your cheekbone sits. These two women have the exact same cheekbone structure and are a likely match."

"It's what we call in the trade a lifelong look. Even through the aging process, a person generally keeps the same shape of their head. There's nothing in these photos that tells me this is not Sister Helen, and there's certainly a lot of information that suggests it is."

I was pleased with the results of the analysis. As Mancusi explained to me, there aren't a lot of absolutes in his line of work, but I definitely had very significant data pointing in my favor. I would now have to decide exactly how to end my journey. I knew I had done enough digging and had enough footage to make the film I wanted to make. But after having come so far emotionally and mentally, that wasn't enough. I needed to do what my parents had suggested—find a definitive way to explain the truth.

NINETEEN

New Mexico

T he final thing I needed to do was film an interview with one of the sisters who knew Helen personally. I was going to the New Mexico convent to do just that. But it wasn't going to be easy. As helpful as Sister Seraphine had been up to this point, she balked when I mentioned heading out to the convent with a camera.

"I don't think that's a good idea at all," she told me on the phone. "We devote our lives to religious matters. We don't appear in films."

She told me that if I showed up at the convent, she wouldn't let me in. But I had gone too far to back down now. I'd deal with Sister Seraphine when I got to New Mexico. Mancusi's work was impressive, but I still felt there was no substitute for a firsthand, positive ID confirming that Sister Helen was the woman in *Pafko at the Wall*.

I dug into my own pocket to pay for the trip for me and one tech guy, David, who could operate the camera and set up the sound. I knew from my near-arrest in New Jersey that showing up at a convent uninvited might draw the attention of the police, but I didn't care: This was something I had to do. I was one step away from solving the greatest mystery in the history of sports. I wouldn't be able to live with myself if I hadn't at least *tried* to achieve this last part of my quest.

I first drove to the convent alone just to get the lay of the land. The roads were paved with gray cement, different from the black-top I was expecting. I noticed the long stretches between traffic lights and the big, beautiful mountains surrounding me on all sides. Following the directions for the convent, I turned off the main road into a sterile, semiresidential community that looked almost like a ghost town. The buildings were ranch style and well kept. The roadsides were covered in sandy dirt that blew onto the windshield as I drove along the three miles to my destination.

The convent sat off a small gravel road with nary a person or car in sight. As I drove along, I noticed a sign that read: BASEBALL BEFORE DRUGS. Why in the world would that sign be fifty yards from a convent in an empty New Mexico town? I took it as a good if slightly strange omen.

I parked the car under a tree across the road from the convent and just sat and watched. The sun was nearly blinding, reflecting off the white stuccoed stone walls of the building. The front entrance had a small parking area right outside of it. If I drove over there, I knew I'd be spotted immediately—there was nowhere to hide. So I just watched from across the way.

I called my dad.

"I'm here," I said calmly into the phone.

"What's it like?" he asked.

"It's creepy. There's no one around."

I told him about the baseball sign. He just laughed.

"If they call the cops, you're screwed."

I knew he was right. But I also knew that what I needed was right inside the convent. How could I *not* go in? A new idea came to me. I worried that the direct approach of just knocking on the door would put the sisters too much on the defensive. The next day, I'd return with David, wait outside once again, and try to show *Pafko at the Wall* to the sisters as they came and went from the convent. That way, I'd get what I needed and get out of there.

I had so much nervous energy I could hardly sleep that night. I got out of bed early the next morning, feeling fearless. David and I drove back and parked in the exact same spot. Even though it was only ten o'clock in the morning, it was extremely hot outside, and we sat in the car with the air-conditioning on max, waiting for a sister to walk through the large wood doors. The convent parking lot was nearly empty again. An hour passed, and I started to get nervous. My mind was racing with fears that maybe the convent was closed, shut down for good. Just then, I saw the heavy wood door slowly creep open. A nun dressed in an ankle-length black robe and full black habit gingerly walked out and headed straight for the flower garden—a few paces from the front door.

I didn't know what to do so I just watched her. For all I knew, she was Sister Seraphine. I hoped that if she saw me in person, she'd know how serious I was about my mission and maybe soften her stance. I had no choice. I opened the car door and walked across the road past the threshold of the convent entrance. As I approached, I saw that the sister was elderly, maybe ninety years old.

"Good morning, Sister. What lovely flowers you have here," I commented, pointing to the white, star-shaped blossoms.

"Oh, thank you. They're yuccas," she responded.

I thought I recognized her voice, "Are you Sister Seraphine, by any chance?"

"I'm Sister Margaret. Sister Seraphine is on a retreat today. But Sister Patricia is covering for her. Is there something I could help you with?"

I remembered Sister Seraphine telling me that Sister Patricia was the one who had known Sister Helen the best.

"Actually, I would like to have a word with Sister Patricia," I offered, careful to not mention anything about filming the conversation.

Pointing at the wood doors, she told me, "She's right inside there at the front desk."

I brought my palms together in prayer and thanked her for her help. Then I walked quickly back to the car to tell David what was happening. I figured he could walk in beside me with the camera and shoot what we needed.

"Dave, you're not going to believe this. The nun who knew Sister Helen best is right behind those doors."

David's eyes scanned the parking lot. He had heard stories from his girlfriend, who was born in the Southwest, about how tough the New Mexico police were—particularly on people not from around there. He was not as brazen as I, but then again, it wasn't his fight.

"What if the cops come?" he asked.

"If they come, they come. We may never get this opportunity again. I'm going in. If you're with me, grab your gear."

I climbed out of the car and headed toward the convent, David nervously trailing me with the camera. I wrapped my hand around the thick wooden handle and pulled the door open.

The first thing I saw inside, hanging on the wall, was a large statue of Jesus on the cross, crown of thorns and all. The room was dark and sparse. Barely able to see because of the change in light, I could just make out an old metal desk, with an even older-looking desk lamp, sitting right in the middle of the room.

I heard a gentle voice: "Can I help you?"

There she was: Sister Patricia. She was a heavy-set woman in her late seventies with gray hair, dressed in a black top with a large wooden crucifix around her neck. I calmly approached the desk, as David started filming from the doorway. It was a run-and-gun shoot. He switched to manual iris and opened the setting as high as it would go without losing picture. Fortunately, between the desk lamp and the backlighting from inside the convent, we had just enough light.

"Good morning, Sister. My name is Brian Biegel."

I told her that I had spoken to Sister Seraphine on the phone several times and that she had mentioned her name. She recalled speaking to Sister Seraphine about Sister Helen Rita and was happy to talk about what she remembered.

"I was Sister Helen Rita's mother superior for a short while before she passed away," said Sister Patricia.

I told her the whole story about the miracle ball.

"I don't remember ever seeing her with a baseball," she told me, "but she loved the game. She used to listen to the games on the radio all the time in her room. I could hear it. Our rooms were close to one another. She never talked about it. But I knew."

"So you don't have any idea what might have happened to the ball?"

"Maybe she gave it to a student as a reward. Or maybe she kept it hidden."

"Do you ever remember her talking about her sister, Genevieve?"

"She'd talk about her all the time. She told me she used to go visit Genevieve in New York City before she transferred out here. That was a long time ago," she said with a chuckle.

"How about the way she conducted herself? I mean, was she a shy person, an outgoing person . . . ?"

Leaning forward in her chair, suddenly Patricia became more serious.

"She liked her authority. She was kind of bossy, to tell you the truth. But a very dedicated person."

I had heard enough. It was time for the moment of truth. From the time I'd come into possession of *Pafko at the Wall* nearly two years ago, it had paid many dividends. But none could be bigger than what I was trying to accomplish now. I asked Sister Patricia if she'd be kind enough to look at an old photograph. I took *Pafko at the Wall* out of my trusty white cardboard envelope and placed it in her hands. She smiled as if I might be kidding. But I had never been more serious. Sister Patricia glanced down at the picture.

"You flew all the way out here from New York for *this*?"

I nodded. She leaned back in her chair, still looking surprised. Then she placed her eyeglasses onto the bridge of her nose, raising them from a chain dangling from her neck. She held the oversize photo in front of her face.

"What year is this from?"

"Nineteen fifty-one."

I noticed that her eyes were glancing all around the picture and she was confused, so I made a small circle with my finger in the area where the ball was, asking her to concentrate there.

Sister Patricia slid the photo under the old desk lamp. Now she leaned forward in her seat. Out of the corner of my eye, I saw that David's terry-cloth headband could no longer absorb his sweat. It was pouring down his face. What I felt on the inside, he was showing on the outside.

After a long and silent examination of the photograph, Sister Patricia was ready to speak. She gently placed her finger beneath our suspect and said with a hint of amazement, "You know, that could be Sister Helen Rita. Right there."

"Could be" were not exactly the words I wanted to hear. She looked closer at the photo and tried angling it toward the light.

"It's so hard to see. But I wouldn't say it's not her. I wish the face was bigger."

"Actually, Sister, that can be arranged."

I pulled out my laptop and placed it on her desk.

Nearly two years had passed since I'd begun my quest to find out what really happened to the Shot Heard 'Round the World. In the end, the road led me here, to a dusty convent in New Mexico on a steamy hot Friday morning. I opened the photo and zoomed in 150 percent. Sister Patricia was now completely focused. She never took her eyes off the screen. She just sat there in deep thought for a good ten seconds. Her next words made my heart soar:

"Oh, my goodness. That's her. Yes, that's her. That's Sister Helen Rita."

She looked away from the screen and pointed directly at Helen in the photo, still on the desk in front of her.

I thanked Sister Patricia. I no longer had even a scintilla of doubt.

While David stood there marveling with Sister Patricia about the photograph, I drifted off into another dimension, wandering out of the convent without uttering a word. I fought back tears and made my way back to the rental car, trying to absorb what had just happened. I looked back at the convent and knew that my job was nearly complete. I picked up my cell phone and dialed my dad. Before it even rang, I hung up. I didn't know what to say to him. I knew he'd be happy for me, but part of me didn't want this journey to end. I had experienced many ups and downs since that trip across the Fifty-ninth Street Bridge with my dad twenty-three months ago, but despite all the starts and stops along the way, the search for the ball had given me much more than it had taken away. I felt a real connection to the world around me, especially to my parents, and my life had meaning again. Suddenly a rush of adrenaline kicked in. I picked up my cell again and hit redial. He picked up on the first ring.

"What's the latest?"

Then, like a boy who just hit a game-winning home run to lead his Little League team to victory, I yelled into the phone, "I did it, Dad!" My pace quickened: "I did it, I did it, I did it!"

I remember exactly what he said.

"You found the ball?"

"Better, Dad. I found the truth."

Faith

I will never know the details for certain, but I created a scenario in my mind of what exactly might have happened to Sister Helen in the days surrounding the game:

I imagined Sister Helen as a Giants fan—she spent many years in New York State, and the Giants were rooted in history as the oldest professional baseball team from New York. I pictured her following the team throughout 1951, paying close attention to their amazing comeback, listening to the games on a radio in her room. As the summer stretched out, the Giants made their move, closing the gap on the Dodgers as the rookie Willie Mays showed he was for real, and Bobby Thomson—reinvented as a third baseman—found power in his bat that he didn't know he still had. The Giants caught the Dodgers on the last day of the season, shocking the sports world and thrilling Sister Helen.

The Giants won game one of the best-of-three playoff series and stood at the threshold. Sister Helen promised herself that if there was to be a game three, she'd be there, to root her team on in person. She was disappointed after the Dodgers won game two, but she was undaunted. She put her plan into play—she'd travel from

Sister Helen Rita. *Courtesy of the Felician Sisters*

Buffalo's Railway Express station at Curtiss Street, riding the number 32 express train to New York City in time for the next day's game.

Aboard the train, looking out the window as she cruised by miles and miles of western New York countryside, Sister Helen prayed that her team had one last miracle in them. The next morning—a cloudy and dank day—she left her sister's apartment and traveled a short distance to the ballpark. She arrived at the horseshoe-shaped stadium in time to purchase one of the only tickets still available—a bleacher seat—for sixty cents. She got her ticket and made her way through the tunnel and up the ramp out to section 35, dressed like an ordinary fan. She sat there in anticipation, as the action spread out on the field before her.

By the bottom of the ninth, many Giants fans had accepted defeat. They were down three runs to a good team; maybe it wasn't meant to be. But Sister Helen *wouldn't give up. She was a woman of faith. She watched with awe, but not sur-prise, as they mounted their comeback—the first run coming off workhorse pitcher Don Newcombe before he was relieved by Ralph Branca.*

When Thomson stepped to the plate, she closed her eyes and prayed. They opened to the crack of the bat and a roar from the crowd. From her angle, she knew it was headed to the seats. Pafko didn't stand a chance. The ball was hooking pretty far to her right, so she had no reflex to try to catch it. She followed the flight of the ball as it headed for the glove of the bushy-haired man who'd been screaming all game. She didn't think about the ball; she was just so happy that her faith had been rewarded. But the ball hit the man's glove, and ricocheted left. It bounced directly to her and, wide-eyed, she grabbed it.

Acknowledgments

To sister Rebecca. You're a guiding light toward a world filled with hope and prosperity. You've been a constant source of wisdom, love, happiness, and inspiration. There's no one who appreciates good news like you, Rebecca. I wouldn't be where I am without you.

To Steve, big brother and mentor. Our bond is unbreakable and will last forever. Your efforts helping me discover certain facts that appear in the book, particularly about Saint Rita, were invaluable. My sincere thanks to you, Hup.

To Bob Makela, a soul from a world we all should aspire to live in. I'd need thirteen pages to describe how much emotional generosity, kindness, and positive energy you've supplied me with over the years. Your editorial notes for the narration of the film were brilliant and aided in retelling the story for this book as well.

To Jackie and Jordan. Thanks for your patience.

To Anthony DeRiso. You're one of my oldest and closest friends, who I know I can always count on!

To Susan Watts. There aren't enough ways I can express how much respect, appreciation, and gratitude I have toward you for helping me through this journey. You truly rock, Suzie Cakes!

To Pete Fornatale. If collaboration means two people coming together to achieve one common goal, then I want my future career goals to be met with you by my side.

To (little) Dom Frandina. You're truly a friend for life. I've leaned on you in the past and you've always come through without expecting anything in return.

To Scott Waxman. You not only saw the value and possibility in this story, but you helped shape it as well. You are indeed a fantastic literary mind, agent, and visionary. The publishing industry needs to take a page out of your book, Scott.

To everyone involved in working on the film, notably my partners, Sal Del Giudice and Scott Weitz. All the thanks in the world!

To Jed Donahue and Brett Valley. Your editorial expertise and ability to see the vision of the book helped shape a story that hopefully makes people feel inspired and entertained.

To Scott Jaffe. For many years you've been a great friend and I'm happy to return the favor as your personal Dallas Cowboys therapist.

To Dan Austin and Hal Sherman. Two of New York's finest from the past, present, and future. Couldn't have done it without you guys.

To Brendan Kahn and his wonderful family. My sincere thanks for staying the course and helping right to the end.

And finally, to Jack Biegel. Poppa, there's no way I could ever thank you enough for being the caring and devoted father that you are. It'd be impossible to even try. But here goes: As a little kid you taught me never to back down from anyone or anything. As a teenager you taught me the difference between right and wrong. And as an adult you became my best friend and always believed in me more than I did myself. Then when life threw me an unhittable curveball, and the universe tested my resolve, you still never gave up

on me. Ever! You can't even imagine how meaningful and powerful one short sentence was whenever I struggled to simply survive:
"You have to be strong, Brian" were the exact words you'd continu-
ally tell me. You can't know how purposeful those six words were.
They penetrated my brain more than any medication ever did. I
love you with every ounce of my existence, Dad. Mommy is looking
down at you and seeing what a great man you truly are.

Others I would like to thank: Ted Spencer, Brad Horn, Freddy
Berowski, and Pat Kelly at the Baseball Hall of Fame; Michael
O'Keeffe, Vic Ziegel, and Claus Gugelberger at the *New York Daily
News;* Sal Marchiano, Lolita Lopez, and Bob Taute at WBII; Dr.
Ilene Donin, Dr. David Kaufman, and Dr. Howard Hao; Larry
Rosen; Richard Propper at Solid Entertainment; Rob Luttrell,
Neil Murphy, and Jim Finn at Heavy Light Digital; Larry and Joy
Haber; James and Kristen Spina; Monsignor Thomas Hartman;
Bobby Dallas; Ken Farber; Sean Cassidy at Dan Klores Associ-
ates; Rob Neyer at ESPN; Byrd Leavell, Melissa Sarver, and every-
one else at the Waxman Literary Agency; Steven Malk at Writers
House; Cory Melious, Marshall Grupp, and Travis Call at Sound
Lounge; Susan Van Metre; the folks at Scarlet Heifer Advertising;
Joseph and Louis Brancato; family members Melissa, Samara, and
Mitch Klafter and Julia, Cameron, and Nina Biegel.

About the Authors

BRIAN BIEGEL is an award-winning writer and filmmaker whose credits include *Getting My Child Back: Fighting Autism* and the documentary film *Miracle Ball,* based on his book of the same name. He has written and produced on-air promotions for ABC and USA television. He lives in Manhattan.

PETER THOMAS FORNATALE is a freelance writer and editor. His most recent collaboration, *A Lion's Tale: Around the World in Spandex,* written with Chris Jericho, was a *New York Times* bestseller. He lives in Brooklyn, New York.